THE
BOUZOUKI
BOOK

**A workshop guide to building
Irish bouzoukis and citterns
by
Graham McDonald**

Copyright © 2004 by Graham McDonald
Published by Graham McDonald Stringed Instruments
PO Box 365, Jamison
ACT, 2614, Australia

First printed June, 2004

ISBN 978-0-646-43602-9

National Library of Australia Cataloguing-in-Publication data

McDonald, Graham.
The Bouzouki Book : a workshop guide to building Irish bouzoukis
and citterns.
ISBN 978-0-646-43602-9
 1. Musical instruments - Construction. 2. Bouzouki -
Construction. 3. Cittern - Construction. 4. Musical
 instruments - Ireland. I. Title.

784.1923

ACKNOWLEDGEMENTS

Thank you to everyone who has encouraged this project over several years with special mention to:

My fellow luthiers Jim Williams, Gerard Gilet, Graham Caldersmith, Doug Eaton. Scott Wise and Phill Kearney who read the manuscript and made helpful comments and suggestions;

Bob Hefner who edited the copy and sorted out all my apostrophes, hyphens, commas and semi-colons;

Julie Bradley who offered lots of good ideas on layout and design;

Andy Irvine for his kind words in the forward;

The customers who have bought my instruments over the years and;

My wife Lynn and the rest of my family; Brendan, Kirsty, Davy and Purdy the dog who is the guardian of the workshop, who have all put up with sometimes obsessional behaviour as this book has taken shape.

Australia Council
for the Arts

arts**ACT**
ACT URBAN SERVICES

This book has been written and pubished with the assistance of the Commonwealth Government through the Australia Council, its funding and advisory body and; the ACT Government through its Cultural Council and ArtsACT.

This page is blank

CONTENTS

This page is blank

FORWARD

s someone who was pretty close to the birth of the
bouzouki in Ireland, I feel I know a little about it's history.

If Johnny Moynihan had taken our advice that evening in
Galway, so long ago, the instrument would have died in
childbirth. Fortunately, he was not the kind of man to take
that sort of advice!

As Graham will tell you, by quirks of fate and hostages to
fortune, Johnny discarded his original Greek bouzouki having
found a flat backed one. The story as I remember it, was that
a man called Bailey had made it for someone who never
came to collect it and Johnny duly bought it. How would the
course of Irish music have run, we have always wondered, if
that man - was it John Pearse - had collected his instrument
before Johnny got wind of it.....

I was shortly to be in a band with Johnny, called Sweeney's
Men and got to play his bouzouki when he was playingtin
whistle, or not looking. I didn't get on with it too well, initially,
preferring to play the Gibson A3 mandolin that the same
Johnny had swapped with me for a fiddle. It took a couple of
years before it finally became my main instrument but I have
explored its possibilities with fascination since about 1968.

photo by Shigeru Suzuki

One thing is for certain though, I know absolutely nothing
about how to make one!

Graham McDonald has been building bouzoukis/citterns/
octave mandolins for over twenty years and should know
a bit about it! He uses lovely native Australian woods and
his instruments are much sought after. In this book, he tells
would-be builders all the tricks of his trade.

So get your band saws and planes out, your fret wire and inlay
and make your own bouzouki!

(Just don't call it a bouzouki when Greeks are about
though....)

Andy Irvine
Jan 2004

This page is blank

Back in 1972 my friend Roger Hargraves rang me up and told me about a new LP he had just picked up from the import record shop in Sydney by a band from Ireland called Planxty. Listening to that recording the first time changed the whole way I thought about how music could be played and especially how folk songs and dance tunes could be accompanied.

Planxty had two members who played double strung instruments. Andy Irvine played mandolin and mandola while Donal Lunny played bouzouki and it was the sound of these instruments intertwining which was so captivating as much as anything else.

One thing led to another and eventually I had a go at building a bouzouki, armed with little else than a photo on a Planxty record cover and Irving Sloan's book on building classical guitars. I discovered that the process of building that first instrument was really as much if not more fun than actually playing it, so I made another, then a guitar, a mandolin and then ended up working with Jim Williams for a couple of years whose guitar building methodology still permeates my approach to building musical instruments.

Over the years the flat-backed Irish bouzouki, the cittern and octave mandolin have infiltrated themselves across the whole range of popular music. There can scarcely be an Irish or Scottish folk band without one and they regularly can be heard on lots of country and pop recordings as an extra tonal colour.

There is little standardization in shape, string length or tuning and while this is part of the instrument's charm it might have something to do with why so little has been written about them. This book tries to cover as much ground as possible, providing information and instructions on building two specific instruments of the bouzouki/cittern/octave mandolin family.

It will cover building both a flat-top/pin bridge long scale - 660mm (26") - bouzouki and an arch-top/floating bridge short scale - 560mm (22") - scale cittern, with enough theoretical background to enable the builder to expand on that to be able to create a range of double strung instruments. In effect, it will be a cookbook, with basic techniques that will be able to be 'mixed and matched'

There will, I hope, be enough for the first-time instrument maker to build a creditable instrument, as well as sufficient detail for the experienced guitar or mandolin maker to be able to branch out in a different direction.

The book pre-supposes some knowledge of timber and the use of woodworking tools. I am not going to tell you how to sharpen a chisel or set a scraper blade. Nor do I go into detail about timber milling and why you should use quarter sawn timber. There are enough specialist 'tone-wood' suppliers for the purchaser to be fairly certain of getting their raw material supplied in the right way.

The methods, tools and jigs are fairly 'low-tech', but do use a number of both stationary and hand-held power tools in addition to common woodworking and specialist lutherie tools. These are detailed in the section on tools and materials. This is not a book where every process is expected to be done only with handtools in some purist, romantic way, but neither are you expected to own a CNC router.

The evolution of a family of instruments

The original citterns had two periods of popularity, firstly in Elizabethan times as instruments of popular music. They were double or triple strung with wire strings, usually with a re-entrant tuning (like a ukulele or 5 string banjo) because the wire making technologies of the day didn't allow wound strings. Anthony Baines, in *European & American Musical Instruments*, suggests that they were a "cheerful strumming or accompanying instrument on which the strings seldom break and are able to keep their tuning pretty well when the instrument is idle." Scale length was usually between 46-54cm (18-21"). They had a couple of unusual features in that the body often got thinner towards the end of the instrument where the strings were attached, and the cross-section of the neck was very asymmetrical, being much thicker on the treble side.

By the end of the 17th century they were out of fashion, except in Germany where they continued as a folk instrument, the waldzither. The middle of the 18th century saw the cittern's re-emergence as a much more robust instrument, which became known as the English guitar. They were briefly fashionable as a parlour instrument in England and France but survived in Portugal, becoming the guitarra, in which form they are an integral part of fado music. Whether the English guitar descended from some ancient Portuguese instrument, or English instruments travelled to Portugal is still debated.

Meanwhile at the other end of Europe and south-western Asia there developed another group of long-necked instruments which evolved into the modern Turkish baglama saz, the Bulgarian tamburitza and several other variants. The saz typically has the body carved from a single piece of wood, with a long neck with three courses of strings tuned g d a, sometimes with three wire strings per course including an octave string, very lightly strung and up to 17 frets to the octave. (No, I don't understand that either, but I have seen several.)

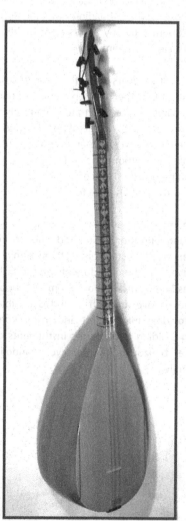

A modern reproduction of a 16th century Italian cittern

A Turkish balama saz with 17 frets to the octave

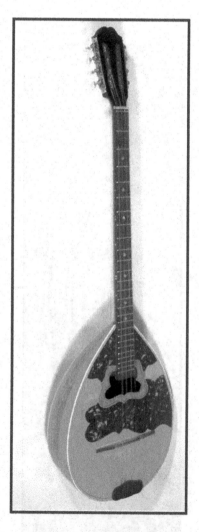

A Greek four-course bouzouki

Pre-20th century Greek bouzoukis were similarly built instruments, until around 100 years ago Greek makers were inspired by the Italian system of staved, bowl back mandolin and mandola construction (which of course goes back to lute building) and they added fixed metal frets instead of the tied on gut of the baglama saz. A tuning of Dad, or equivalent became the most common. A fourth course of strings was added in the 1950s (apparently by Manis Hiotis, a Greek tenor banjo player) and a CFad tuning became the norm. This is the top four strings of a guitar tuned down two semitones.

As is the nature of such things, musical tourists started bringing Greek bouzoukis back home from holidays and Irish musicians started experimenting with them. Andy Irvine remembers a session in Galway in 1966 where Johnny Moynihan, with whom Andy played in Sweeney's Men, with a Greek bouzouki and joining in. Andy remembers the instrument as being a horrible, out of tune thing and Johnny was told strongly to go somewhere else with it. Shortly afterwards Moynihan purchased from John Pearse a flat backed bouzouki that had been commissioned from luthier John Bailey, which had ended up being flat-backed because Bailey (according to Pearse) didn't know how to make a bowl back.

Moynihan strung the instrument with unison strings and used a GDad tuning which he and Irvine had been using on mandolins. Andy ended up with a Greek instrument himself and when Donal Lunny visited his flat a year or so later Donal ended up going home with it after playing it for some hours upside down. He re-strung it left-handed with unison strings and adopted the GDad tuning as well.

As anyone who has ever played one knows, the bowl back of the Greek instrument makes it quite hard to play standing up, and in 1970 Donal commissioned luthier Peter Abnett to make another flat backed version which has become the best known instrument of its type.

This brief history is mostly from Andy's recollections, along with a letter John Pearse wrote to the *American Lutherie* following an article I had written on the Irish bouzouki, and various interviews that have been published over the years. There is doubtless some detail lost in the mists of time, but in any case, Johnny Moynihan, John Pearse, Donal Lunny and Andy Irvine have all had a vital role in the instrument's development.

In 1973 English luthier Stefan Sobell created a five course instrument which he dubbed a cittern. As I mentioned previously, the original cittern was first popular in Elizabethan times, and then had a revival in the late eighteenth century from whence it evolved into the Portuguese guitarra, a short scale 6 course instrument with a floating bridge used as an accompaniment for singing. Sobell's design owes a lot to the Portuguese instrument combined with a Martin arch-top guitar from the '30s so he decided to call his creations a cittern. These modern citterns are usually a shorter scale - 530-610mm (21-24") - than bouzoukis and a range of tunings are commonly used although commonly utilising 5ths between courses.

Johnny Moynihan around 1967, with what may well be the very first Irish bouzouki

Greek bouzoukis typically have a scale length of 660-685mm (26-27"), which makes for a big stretch for those playing melody lines in lower positions, and so shorter scale versions of the Irish bouzouki have been built as well, usually in the 530-560mm (21-22") range, similar to a tenor banjo. These are usually known as octave mandolins. Also common in European mandolin orchestras is the octave mandola, tuned an octave below a mandolin, but with a short scale, often around 400mm (16"). This is the same scale length as the Gibson mandola usually tuned CGda'. Several of the American mandolin manufacturers also made octave mandolin style instruments in addition to the more common mandolin orchestra instruments of mandolin, mandola and mando-cello, but they were never very popular although quite a number of mando-cellos have ended up being recycled with octave mandolin/bouzouki tuning.

Nomenclature

There is ongoing discussion about what to call this family of instruments, but there now seems to be a slowly forming consensus that long scale (24"/600mm and up) four course instruments are 'bouzoukis', short scale (21 -22"/530-560mm) four course instruments are 'octave mandolins' and short scale five course models are 'citterns'. A long scale five course gets called whatever the maker wants to call it, though 'five course bouzouki' or 'long scale cittern' is common.

One small complication is that in Europe, 'octave mandolins' are often refered to as 'octave mandolas', and what is called a mandola on the US is refered to as a 'tenor mandola' in Europe.

Tunings

Along with the range of scale lengths and numbers of strings, there are also a bewildering number of tunings used. For four course instruments the most common are GDad and GDae (an octave down from a mandolin) with ADad or AEae also used. With five course instruments GDaea' or GDadg are frequently used along with others like GDgdg. These five course tunings add the extra course as higher strings, but there is also the approach of adding a lower fifth course tuned to D or even C. Adding a string at these lower pitches requires a longer scale length, at least 610mm (24") for reasons of string gauge and tension.

The next chapter on designing a bouzouki or cittern will explore string tensions and finding the appropriate strings for a particular tuning.

Measurements in this book

While most of the world uses the metric system these days, America is still resolutely fixed to the old Imperial system of feet and inches. I tend to use both, often for measuring different things. Most of the measurements will be in metric because it is just simpler to use most of the time, but there are things that I have always thought of in Imperial for one reason or another and the Imperial measurement will be there for a reason. Scale lengths I think of in inches, but metric equivalents will be given.

In some areas, such as building truss-rods for the instruments neck, I use 3/16" steel rod - which is not the same as 5mm- and 10-32 threadcutting dies and nuts, because these are the components which are readily available from suppliers. For measuring string action -the height of the string above the frets - I use 64ths of an inch because that was the way I was taught by Jim Williams over 20 years ago, and it is a good increment to work in though 1000ths of an inch is equally useful. (For those interested, a 64th of an inch is about .4mm) Plain steel and bronze wound strings are usually sold with the diameter of the strings measured in 1000ths of an inch. There is, however, a metric-imperial conversion chart as Appendix 1.

A 26"-660mm scale flat-top bouzouki

When building a guitar, the maker usually has to work within a fairly strict set of parameters. There are industry standards for scale length, and general expectations of the proportions of the body shape, though still plenty of scope for individuality and adventurous design ideas. With bouzoukis/ citterns/octave mandolins there are fewer expectations of the 'correct' way of going about creating such an instrument, though most instruments in the family use a mandolin style teardrop shaped body. What is often referred to a 'the onion on a stick' design.

The plans at the back of the book contain templates for a body shape, bracing pattern, side width, head shape and other bits and pieces, but there is lots of scope for variation.

One design factor to consider is what the player is used to. A customer pointed out to me some years ago that he found that bouzouki/cittern players who had come to the instrument from the mandolin often preferred an arch-top/floating bridge instrument, while guitar players were more comfortable with a fixed, pin bridge instrument.

Variables

Bouzoukis are primarily played with a flatpick, though there are fingerpickers out there. Styles range from straight melodic playing, to chordal rhythm or a mixture of both. Melody players tend to prefer a shorter scale instrument. I suggest a 560mm (22") scale which conveniently is the 24 27/32" short scale Gibson scale, starting on the second fret or the third fret on the 26 1/8" long scale classical on the Ibex Fret Ruler. A number of builders use a shorter scale - 510 -535mm (20-21") - for octave mandolin or cittern, but I think that the strings necessary are outside the 'optimal range' for those pitches.

McDonald's Unified Theory on Stringing - For any particular pitch and string length, there is a narrow range of strings that can be practically used.

For example, an acoustic guitar first string tuned to e needs to be somewhere between a .010" and .013" which are the standard gauges for extra-light and medium guitar sets. On a 650mm (25.5") scale guitar the .010" has a tension of around 7.5 kg (16.5 lbs) and the .013" string has a tension of a little less than 12.2kg (26.8lbs).

Any lighter on an acoustic guitar and it will rattle around on the frets and won't drive the soundboard because the tension is too low (for a .008" string the tension goes down to around 4.7 kgs) and anything over a .014" would be really hard to play, and would be getting close to putting too much tension on the instrument. A light gauge set of guitar strings will be putting around 60-70kg of tension on the instrument, with a medium set increasing that to around 80kg.

The extension of this theory is that within the usable range of strings the lighter in gauge you can go for a given pitch, the more overtones and harmonic richness there will be in the sound produced. As an example a .040" G string on a 660mm (26") scale instrument makes a more complex and interesting sound than a .046" G string on a 560mm (22") instrument though the tensions are quite similar. This is why I am suggesting that going to a 510-535mm (20-21") scale instrument will need even thicker strings, with even more loss of tonal quality. An even more extreme example of this is the octave mandolas used in European classical mandolin ensembles. They use a scale around 400mm (16") and need huge wound strings to get the necessary tension and make a sound like 'plodge'.

For bouzoukis I prefer tensions of between 7-10kg per string, giving a total tension of between 70 and 80 kg which is similar to a guitar. The formula and charts in Appendix 2 allows quick calculation of appropriate strings for particular tunings. What can also be quickly found out is what tunings won't work. For the usual four course tunings there are not many problems. It is when adding a fifth course, either higher or lower, that it can be tricky such as trying to put a low D string on a 535mm (21") scale or a high A on a 660mm (26") scale instrument.

For a more chordal player, a longer scale that uses lighter strings gives a sound with more overtones in the sound. Any standard guitar scale works fine, with my preference the relatively long 660mm (26") scale. Using a standard guitar scale has the advantage of being able to purchase a thicknessed and slotted fretboard from an number of suppliers. Slotting fretboards is, I'm sure, good for the soul, and will be covered in a later chapter, but it can make sense to buy one ready made.

Scale length will also determine what tuning can be used on a five course instrument. A short scale instrument can add a high g or a string, but adding a low D means a very heavy gauge string. Similarly it is impractical to add a high string to a long scale instrument, but a low D becomes quite a reasonable proposition, though with some thought given to body size. Consideration has to be given to the resonances of the instrument's body in comparison to those with a G as the lowest string.

The Neck

The parameters of the neck - scale length, number of strings, width and number of frets - are going to determine various elements of the rest of the instrument. In the introduction I mentioned the relationship between tunings and scale length, keeping in mind the practicalities of any particular combination.

A nut width of 34mm for a four course instrument is comfortable for most players, though I have made the nuts up to 40mm wide, and as narrow as 30mm. For a five course instrument with an added high course, a width of 42mm allows the same spacing between courses and for a five course instrument with the extra strings on the bottom a nut width of 44mm is called for.

For the 34mm nut the width at the 12th fret is 44mm, for the 42mm nut 54mm at the 12th fret, and 56mm for the 44mm nut. This will give a similar flare to the line of the strings as a steel string guitar.

The size of the headstock must also be considered. Making a four course instrument there is the choice of either 4-on-a-plate mandolin tuners, or individual machine heads, preferably with small buttons. The only decent quality standard (ie not for Gibson F style heads) mandolin tuners are those by Schaller which require a 23mm spacing. Individual machines heads with small buttons will require a minimum of 27mm spacing so they don't interfere with each other and can be adjusted separately. The shape of the headstock itself can be as individualistic as you like, but mine are tapered from the widest point, 25mm from the nut, of 70mm down to 40mm at the end. Total length is 180mm. The tapered design means the strings go from the nut to the tuning posts with out interfering with each other and with only a slight deviation from the line of the nut slots.

The Body

Bouzoukis have no real limitations on the body shape. A scaled up mandolin teardrop shape is the most common, but a small guitar shape works just as well. In some ways even better, as the body of the instrument sits on the leg much more comfortably, and the greater air volume of the body enhances the instrument's bass response. Whatever shape is decided it is important to place the bridge in the centre of the vibrating area. With a teardrop body this is usually around halfway between the soundhole and the bottom of the instrument at its widest point. 5-10mm either way is not going to make much difference, but working out the exact position is important in relationship to the soundboard bracing.

The teardrop body shape included with this book is typical, and places the neck join at the 17th fret for a long - 635mm+ (25"+) - scale four course bouzouki, or at the 13th fret for a short - 560mm (22") - scale cittern or octave mandolin. This size body is a bit too small for adding a lower 5th course. This would need either a larger teardrop or a guitar style body.

Body depth is 85mm at the tail and 75mm at the neck join, which looks about the right proportion for a body 400mm long and 350mm wide.

I suggest building with either a flat-top using a guitar style pin bridge, or an arched top with a higher bridge and tailpiece. I do not recommend instruments with a flat-top and a low floating bridge for a number of structural reasons, though this is the most common way these instruments are built. The chapter on soundboards discusses this more fully.

The instrument needs a soundhole, which is usually at the end of the fretboard, but need not necessarily be there. Nor must it be round. There have been lots of strange and wonderful ideas for soundhole position and shape over the years, but a round soundhole is easier to make. For a teardrop body a hole diameter of 80mm works well, and is big enough to get a reasonably sized hand inside to make adjustments, fit pickups and the like. The 80mm soundhole was arrived at more or less instinctively, looking in proportion to the body size, and importantly, big enough to get my hand inside the instrument's body.

Soundholes need not necessarily be circular, though that is the simplest way to make them, and need not even be just the one. Instruments like the Ovation Adamas have a number of smaller soundholes. The important consideration is the total area of soundhole(s), as this is a critical factor for the resonances of the instrument.

The body of any stringed instrument essentially in a similar way to a ported or vented loudspeaker cabinet, with the soundboard as the speaker cone, the back and sides as a stiffer and more rigid speaker box, and the soundhole as the port.

The research and writings of people like Graham Caldersmith, Al Carruth and others have been published in journals like *American Lutherie*, the quarterly publication of The Guild of American Luthiers. Their writings on guitar resonances, and importantly, what a good guitar's resonances are, can be extrapolated to apply to bouzoukis and citterns, and we will cover that in the chapter on soundboards.

Flat-top or Arch-top

The difference in sound between a flat-top/pin bridge instrument and an arch-top with a floating bridge is subtle but distinct. I am often asked what the difference is, but I have never come up with a definitive answer. The difference is not as great as between an arch-top and a flat-top guitar, partly because arch-top guitar makers are looking for a different sound quality than a flat-top, and my flat-top bracing pattern also shapes the sound differently. The arch-top does have a 'punchier', more immediate sound, while the flat-top sound is a little rounder with more warmth in the bass.

One approach to making arch-tops is not the usual one of carving from a solid piece of wood, but involves moulding wood 7mm thick by heat and steam into the general shape of the arch and then carving that into the usual graduated thickness of a fully carved top. An unusual way of doing it, but it works. There is also a section on fully carving a soundboard.

Laying out the design

If you don't wish to use the included plans for either the long scale four course or short scale five course instruments, a sheet (or two) of stiff card is needed to draft the instrument design. Start a plan drawing by laying out a centre line, marking in the nut, frets and bridge saddle positions for your desired instrument. The bridge saddle will not be exactly twice the nut to 12th fret distance. You will need to add about 3mm to compensate for pushing the strings down to the frets and sharpening the pitch. This will be further explained in the chapter on bridges.

Mark the width at the nut and at the 12th fret according to the measurements given previously and the two lines joining those points will be the width of the fingerboard. The width at the 12th fret will also be the outside string spacing at the saddle.

Add a head to the end of the fingerboard, of whatever shape you want. A slotted design is practical, although it does make it harder to change strings.

At the end of the fingerboard is usually the place for the soundhole. My usual bouzouki soundhole is 80mm, going up to 90mm for a guitar bodied instrument and down to 72mm for a Cgda' tuned mandola.

Around these elements fill in the body shape, remembering that the bridge should be around the widest point of the body. It is easiest to cut a half-body template out of thick card to ensure a symmetrical body shape. Of course there is no real reason to make the body symmetrical. My guitar bodied bouzoukis have the waist on the treble side 12mm (1/2") further back than on the bass side, which allows the waist to flow into the cutaway.

It is also useful to make card templates for the fingerboard shape and the head shape, though not essential.

Building a musical instrument can be done with a minimum of hand tools only, but it would be hard work. Power tools not only do things more quickly, but can often do particular jobs more accurately. Most of the tools and equipment listed below would be in the workshop of a dedicated amateur woodworker, though there are some specialised tools. Most of the jigs will be to be made, but luthiers are well known for spending time making jigs

Q. How many luthiers does it take to change a light-globe?
A. Just the one, but it will take six months to make the jig.

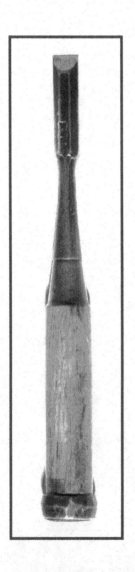

Hand Tools

Chisels - at least 1/4", 3/8", 1/2" & 3/4";
Carving gouges (for archtop) a couple with a number 7 curve is good - at least a 10mm and 18mm. The Pfeil violin gouges are great tools as well;
Sharpening stones (I have a preference for Japanese chisels and water stones, but there are lots of things available) and honing guides;
No 4 smoothing plane;
No 7 shooting plane;
Block plane;
The two larger Ibex violin makers planes or similar - the smaller ones are very cute, but not really useful for instruments bigger than a fiddle;
A small back saw with a replaceable blade. A fine tooth hacksaw blade is good for lots of little jobs;
Exacto or similar hobby knife with replaceable blades;
Scrapers ground to square and 45° edges;
Nut files;
Wooden clothes pegs with rubber bands wrapped around or other small spring clamps for gluing linings;
Large rubber bands for gluing the back.

Clamps, lots of clamps:
Wooden cam clamps are really useful for many jobs and six of each size is a mimimum;
Six 12" bar clamps;
An assortment of G clamps from 1" up to 6".

For fretting:
A fret slotting saw - Stewart McDonald sells one with an acrylic depth guide;
A hammer;
A 30cm medium cut file or carborundum stone (for fret leveling);
1 15-20cm medium file for beveling the fret ends;
A fret crowning file to match the fret wire (2mm is standard);
Ground down carpenters pincers for cutting the fret wire (and pulling them out if you have to).

Workshop supplies

Glues:
Franklin's Titebond - This is the industry standard aliphatic resin wood glue. It is similar in the way it is used to white PVA, but sets up much harder, which is important for jobs like gluing bridges in place. There are several other yellow coloured similar glues on the market, which may work pefectly well, but I know Titebond does.

There are those who swear by using animal glue, which is still used almost exclusively by violin builders. It will provide a bond as good, if not better, than Titebond, but is trickier to use.

Superglue - a tube of cyanoacrylate glue has a multitude of uses. There are a variety of kinds on the market, with the general rule of thumb that the thicker it it (more viscous) the longer it will take to dry. I buy very cheap superglue made in China which comes in blister packs of half a dozen small tubes for a couple of dollars.

Epoxy - small dispenser packs of both 5 minute and regular setup time epoxy

Rubber cement
80, 120, 180, 280 grit aluminium oxide sandpaper
400, 600, 1200 grit wet&dry paper
Cork and hard rubber sanding blocks
Alcohol (Metholated Spirit)
Acetone
18mm masking tape

Hand Power Tools

Electric drill;
Rechargable electric drill (useful for drilling small holes and driving screws);
Router -1HP - I have three - one on a router table, one for binding and heavier work and another smaller model for jobs like bridge slots;
Orbital sander - really good for sanding backs and soundboards;
A Dremel (or similar).

Stationary Power Tools

Essential
Bandsaw - a Taiwanese 14" does most jobs except for resawing large pieces of wood. A 1/4" 6tpi blade will do almost anything necessary;
Drill press (bench drill) - multiple speed with a 3/4HP motor. 3", 2" and 1.5" (75mm, 50mm & 35mm) sleeveless drum sanders are a very worthwhile addition;
Disc sander - Mine is an 8" disc with a 6"x 48" belt sander. 80 grit aluminium oxide paper is glued to the disc with rubber cement.
Useful
A wide (16") drum sander for thicknessing;
A 6" jointer for trueing up neck stock;
A thicknesser for necks, braces and fingerboards;
A small table saw with a fret slotting blade and fretting template.

Jigs

The body assembly workboard - This made from 1/2" plywood in the general shape of the bouzouki body, with radial slots cut in to accept 30mm dowels which are attached using a threaded rod (or lag bolts) and wingnuts which hold the sides in place. Blocks at either end provide clamping support for the neck and tail blocks. A hole drilled in the centre takes the axle for the radiused back sanding dish. A useful addition is a T-nut mounted on the underneath in a hole drilled in the centre of the soundhole position. This can be used with a long bolt and a bar to hold the soundboard in place when gluing to the sides.

The body assembly workboard

The binding channel routing jig

Dished workboards - with a 15' radius for backs and a 25' radius for soundboards. This are made from a circle of 18mm MDF or ply onto which are glued radial strips of 2x1" pine cut to the necessary curve and then faced with a disk of 1/8" (3mm) Masonite. There is a template for the curves in the plans section. The pine strips need to be progressively shortened to fit and the Masonite can be glued in place with go-sticks

A small workboard - a little larger than a soundboard that can be clamped in the vice. This is good for working on soundboards and backs in a number of ways. Mine is made from 25mm (1") ply with a solid block of wood screwed and glued to the underside for mounting in the vice.

Side bender - This is a modification to the famed Fox side bender used for guitar sides. It is a bit simpler, and started out life with two 150w and one 100 w light bulbs for heat. I now use a silicon heating blanket. The concave curve around the neck is formed by the large block and one or two smaller blocks are held by springs

Binding router - an attachment to a router to cut the binding channels.

Kerfing jig - This is a very simple jig which runs in the slot in the bandsaw table and cuts the kerfing slots. A block of wood clamped to the table will stop cutting through the kerfing, so you don't end up with a lot of very short lengths of kerfed lining.

Bridge slotting jig - A router jig that holds a bridge blank for routing the saddle slot. The blank is held in place by a couple of 3/16" bolts, and a 5mm router bit is used to cut the slot. Alternatively an X-Y vice for the drill press can be used for this and other milling jobs

A double-sided shooting board - especially useful if molded arch-tops are made.

A go-stick cabinet - This is an open box made from a frame of 50x100mm (2x4") timber with a solid bottom and top and a number of 10mm (3/8") dowels the same length as the inside height of the cabinet. My sticks are a little under 1200mm (4') long.

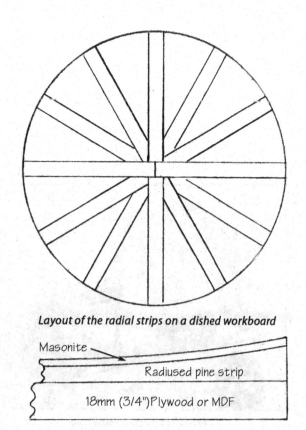

Layout of the radial strips on a dished workboard

Masonite

Radiused pine strip

18mm (3/4") Plywood or MDF

The side bender

Materials

The materials needed for a bouzouki or cittern are essentaially the same as those needed for a small bodied guitar and many suppliers will be able to sell a complete set of materials.

Two bookmatched pieces of Spruce or similar soundboard wood. Sitka spruce is the most commonly used, but there are other spruce varieties as well as western red cedar, redwood, Australian King William and Bunya-Bunya pine. Tone wood suppliers will usually supply this in pieces around 5mm (3/16") thick which is fine for a flat-top instrument. Minmum size is 460mm (18") long by 190mm (7.5") wide if the plans in this book are used. For a molded arch top instrument the two halves need to be 8mm thick, to be reduced to 7mm before molding. For a fully carved archtop the thickest part of the wedge should allow a joined centre thickness of 20mm (13/16")

A set of bookmatched back and sides. As well as the 'standard' timbers such as rosewood and mahogany, there are numerous other species available from specialist suppliers. The wood chosen will have an effect on the final sound of the instrument, but the most expensive materials will not make a bad instrument sound good. The back pieces need to be the same size as the soundboard and the sides can be narrower than those usually supplied for guitars but it will be simpler and easier to buy a set for a small guitar.

A 850mm (33") length of 75x25mm (3x1") quartersawn hardwood for a scarf-jointed neck. Mahogany is the most commonly used timber for necks, but others can be used and might well look more attractive if used with unusal body timbers. If timber such as black walnut, Australian blackwood (black acacia), or maple are used for the body it would make sense to use the same timber for the neck. If a laminated neck is used the requirements will be different.

A fingerboard - usually ebony or rosewood, but other hardwoods can be used.

Fretwire - about 1.2m (4') of wire, 2mm wide is standard

Soundboard braces - usually sold as blocks around 25mm (1") thick from which the braces can be cut. The grain should be as even and straight as possible and cut right on the quarter (the grain running vertically through the 25mm thickness when looked at from the end)

Kerfing - either bought premade or made from strips of mahgany or similar. If made on the bandsaw as described at least six x14" lengths will be needed. Four lengths will be sufficent if bought from a supplier.

Bindings - either wood or plastic - 4x 600mm (24") lengths. Again these can be bought or made from offcuts when trimming the sides to width.

Purflings - either wood or plastic for decoration inside the bindings and around the soundhole

A piece of 2-3mm veneer - 75mm x 200mm (3x10") for the headstock overlay. Depending on the design of the headstock as shorter piece might be sufficient.

A bridge blank from either ebony or rosewood. A blank suitable for a 12-string guitar can be used for the two-piece arch-top bridge.

A tailpiece blank or an arch-top tailpiece if some sort of metal tailpiece is not used.

Bone (or similar) for nut and saddle.

Eight or ten small-button machine heads or a set of mandolin machine heads if a four-course instrument is being made.

And various bits of hardware that will occur in the the book.

The bandsaw jig for slotting kerfing

Humidity

The most critical environmental factor when building a musical instrument is relative humidity. Wood is a hydroscopic material - it absorbs and loses moisture from the air. As it absorbs moisture it expands and shrinks as it loses it. I may have got it wrong, but several years ago I measured the width of a thicknessed soundboard, perhaps 16" (400mm) wide in both dry and very humid conditions. The difference in width was around 2mm. This means that it is vital to do the important gluing operations in dry conditions - around 40% relative humidity - especially the soundboard and back bracing, and when gluing the fretboard to the neck. Humid conditions after the instrument has been glued together will mean that the thin, flat plates of the soundboard and back will swell and dome a little more. Gluing in humid conditions will mean that in low humidity the convex shapes of the plates will shrink to a convexity, or the plates could even split along the grain.

If living in a generally dry climate, it should not be too hard to build instruments in the right humidity. Cheap digital measuring devices are available from electronic shops to check the humidity and temperature. Humid climates will need some humidity control. This can be full airconditioning or an air-tight cupboard fitted with a dehumidifier where the critical glueing jobs can be done.

Router jig for slotting bridges

Slotting a bridge on a drill press with an X/Y sliding vice

Over the years there have developed two main approaches to the way in which Irish bouzoukis and citterns are built. The first is with the flat soundboard (usually somewhat curved laterally though bracing) and a fairly low floating bridge with the strings attached to a tailpiece. The second method uses a carved, arched soundboard, again with a floating bridge, with the arching a little higher than a mandolin.

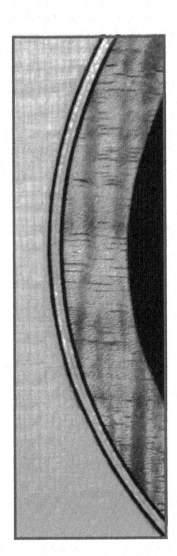

There are a couple of inherent structural problems with the common flat-top bouzouki. The stresses on the body are quite different from a guitar. There are two main stresses at work, the pressure from the tailpiece trying to collapse the body longitudinally, or at least pull the tailpiece up and over towards the machine heads, and the downbearing from the bridge trying to cave-in the soundboard. What tends to happen often is that the soundboard distorts into an 's', with a hump just in front of the tailpiece, a dip underneath the bridge and the headblock rotating bringing the neck up. In the diagram on the following page the dotted lines indicate common body distortions.

Building them with the neck in the same plane as the top (or kicked back only a degree or two) and using a tailpiece, the bridge must necessarily be quite low, and the break angle over the bridge quite shallow. This will mean that the down-pressure on the soundboard is minimised, with the downside of this being that soundboard isn't being driven as hard as it might be, and so volume often suffers. (The loudness of the instrument is often an important consideration for the players, especially of Irish music, because they often spend a good amount of their playing time in sessions trying to hear themselves over the button accordion and bodhran player on either side of them.)

Both archtop guitar and violin builders work on a break angle around 15° over the bridge. This just puts too much down pressure on a flattop instrument, and some degree of structural deformation seems inescapable.

Over several years of building flat-top bouzoukis I tried all manner of approaches to this problem of compressional forces. I played around with the neck angle and bridge height to see what would happen. I took up Greg Smallman's idea of a plywood rim replacing the usual linings and various sorts of flying braces from the tailpiece forward to stiffen the instrument. I finally decided that flat-tops, at least with a floating bridge and tailpiece were not the way to go.

There is also the bending, or cranked top, method where a transverse bend is put in the soundboard just behind the bridge as is usual with Neapolitan mandolins. I built a few of these some years back, routing a groove on the inside of a glued and thicknessed soundboard, and then bending it over a hot pipe. Transverse braces with a reasonable arch were then glued on, and the top attached to the sides with tentalones.

The main reason I experimented with the cranked top was for strength. Putting that bend in the soundboard adds a great deal of strength to offset both the downwards and longitudinal compressional forces at work. Getting the sides and top lined up was a bit tricky, but that's why they invented bindings. (Robert Lundberg's article on mandolins in *American Lutherie* No 46, says that the old makers would bend each half of the soundboard separately and then glue them together. The only excuse I can offer for bending the whole soundboard at one time is that I didn't know any better.)

Flat-top pin-bridge soundboards

I eventually came to the decision that the most practical way of building a bouzouki with a flat top is to use a pin bridge (like 2/3 of a 12-string). A number of makers use this approach, and it does make putting them together a lot easier (especially if you have built guitars), and the sound as I discovered somewhat surprisingly, is not very different from a floating bridge instrument. This is one of the methods described in this book.

The next consideration was the bracing pattern. The bracing in a fixed bridge instrument has the dual purpose of strengthening the soundboard to resist the tension of the strings, but also to stiffen the soundboard so its resonances are at the appropriate frequencies. (This will be covered more fully in the next chapter) There are many bracing patterns in use for steel strung instruments, but most are based upon the venerable Martin X-brace, though the Kasha system of radial bracing has its adherents and Ovation have used a fan design on some of their instruments.

I was looking for a bracing pattern that was going to work a little differently from a guitar type X-brace with the thinking that people would not want a bouzouki that sounded too much like a guitar. In the end I decided that much of the bouzouki sound comes from the double unison (or octave) stringing and the tuning intervals between the strings, but I remembered a 12-string guitar built in the late '80s by Jim Williams using a lattice system of bracing inspired by that of classical guitar builder Greg Smallman. Jim's guitar used a spruce lattice, rather than Greg's carbon-fibre and balsa, but it came from the Smallman idea of a stiff centre of the soundboard with thinner, more flexible edges that was fixed to a rigid body structure.

This small-bodied 12-string was a very loud instrument with remarkable clarity and definition between the notes, rather than the more common 12-string mushiness. The Smallman classical guitars are known for the quick attack of each note and Greg has said that if his soundboards are too stiff the classicals end up sounding more like banjos. Not much good for a classical but it worked for the Williams 12-string and was perhaps applicable for bouzoukis. The end result is my hybrid X-lattice which allows the use of bridge pins while keeping the central stiff zone of the soundboard with a shallow spruce lattice.

Moulded arch-top soundboards

Before I started working on the pin-bridge instruments, I was still very attracted to the idea of floating bridge and tailpiece bouzoukis. The answer to all the structural problems seemed to be carving the tops, in the same way as archtop guitar, or mandolins, but the cost of blocks of spruce big enough for bouzouki tops was pretty high, and at the time I didn't have anything in the way of the necessary gouges and carving chisels, let alone those little violin maker's planes. Then I came across an article in the English magazine, *Early Music*, from the mid '70s describing the restoration of a 16th century viol, and the repairer's discovery that the soundboard appeared to have been bent and then coopered together in four sections, rather like staves of a barrel. He found what looked like scorch marks on the inside where the most radical bends had been made.

The idea of bending the soundboards was appealing for a couple of reasons. Using timber 6-8mm thick rather than 20-25mm was an obvious cost saving, to say nothing of a more efficient use of resources, and the fact that the grain would be running along length of the soundboard's arch would seem structurally stronger.

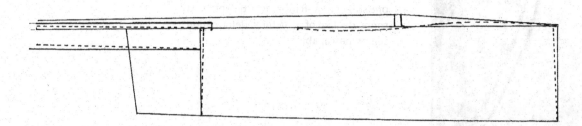

The dotted lines show the deformations that often happens to a flat-top, floating-bridge instrument

It might then be possible to achieve the same structural strength and stiffness with less weight, and so more efficiency in the way the instrument works. If a string has to move less mass in converting the mechanical energy of the string into acoustic energy, then more of that energy can be turned into sound. This is one of the ideas behind Greg Smallman's very light, but stiff classical guitar soundboards.

I later found out that moulding violin soundboards, while not common, has a small but devoted band of adherents, some of whom maintain that this was a method used, perhaps, by Stradivarius, but many of them use a different technique of forcing the arch apart by wedges between the two plates with the outside edges of the shape held together with clamps.

I had a couple of attempts at building coopered soundboards, in the way now adopted by many contemporary builder of viols, but it was quite tricky getting the wood that was around 6mm thick to bend in the quite complicated three dimensional way that was required over a hot pipe, and the shapes were never quite right. This technique was put into the 'interesting, but too hard' basket, and I continued to ponder on ways to form 6mm or more thick pieces of spruce into arched soundboards.

Bending timber needs heat and moisture. I couldn't think of an easy way to heat up pieces of spruce big enough for bouzouki or, for that matter, guitar soundboards while keeping them wet, but I could certainly keep them wet in a large fibreglass tray that I had in the workshop. So I soaked two soundboard halves for a couple of days and clamped them down on a piece of plywood with an 18mm ply hump in the middle, using a ply caul in the shape of the body outline and extending in about 20mm inside the body shape almost to the edge of the hump.

After letting it dry for a few days I took the clamps off, and the arched shape remained, although the spruce sprung back so there was only an 8-10mm internal arch instead of 18mm.

There were still lots of problems to solve, like joining the two halves, and discovering that it was a good idea to plane what would become the inside surfaces before bending. I still wanted to get more arch in the tops, somewhere between a guitar and a mandolin I figured, so longer soaking periods were tried, a double soaking and clamping and a higher hump to bend the wood over. The springback was still there, and trying to bend over the higher hump started to cause some noticeable compression marks in the spruce at the inside edge of the clamping caul where the upward curve started.

Heat was what was wanted as well as the moisture, and I eventually thought of oven bags. They are made by a company called Glad in Australia, and are made of a stiff clear plastic and are used to cook things like chickens and turkeys in the oven to keep them from drying out as they cooked. The bags are good to 200°C which seemed fine for steaming wood. The small problem was that even the biggest ones were not really big enough for a bouzouki soundboard, but they could be cut and opened up into sheets and masking tape held them together and sealed them quite nicely. The size problem was sorted out when I rang the manufacturer, and their PR man said I could have the end of a roll of the material they make the bags out of. The roll was about 400mm wide and doubled over, so a soundboard half fitted in just right, and when the plastic was cut to a length 100mm or so longer than the soundboard half there was plenty to fold over and seal with the masking tape.

The oven in the kitchen was just big enough to hold the wet bits of spruce in their bags, so I fired it up to around 150°C and left them for 20-30 minutes, until I could feel them getting flexible and then onto the mould and clamped up. And it worked even better. There was still some springback, but it was considerably less, and this is the way that this technique has been evolving over the past ten or so years.

It is not a method that I am suggesting should replace fully carved soundboards, but it is an alternative that works remarkably well. The disadvantage is that you can't do some of the interesting sculptural things that you can with a fully carved soundboard as you only have 7mm of wood to start with. The advantage is starting with a lot less wood which, as I am sure we are all aware, is a finite resource, and the inside arch is almost fully formed by the moulding process.

Resonances and why they are important

Most of the character of a stringed instrument is dependent on a complex interaction between the range of the instrument (from lowest open string to the higher notes on the top string) and the behaviour of the soundboard. The soundboard will have particular frequencies where it will vibrate or resonate more strongly than at other frequencies. These resonances are caused by the way a vibrating plate behaves - the way a plate twists and bends - and which is determined by its stiffness and mass. These vibration patterns were first demonstrated by German scientist Ernst Chladni two hundred years ago.

What the thickness and soundboard braces on any wooden stringed instrument are doing is controlling the stiffness of the soundboard. The style of bracing will have some effect by allowing or inhibiting various of the vibrational modes, whether it is a Martin style X- brace, a classical guitar fan, a Kasha radial system or the Smallman lattice, but essentially all bracing is determining the stiffness of the resonating plate.

There are two main ways in which the behaviour of the vibrating parts of a stringed instrument can be measured. One is determining the Chladni patterns of soundboards and backs when they are excited while not attached to the sides - known as 'free plate' testing - and the other driving the finished instrument with a sweep of frequencies to excite the various modes of vibration on a fixed soundboard as well as the way the air within the body resonates as well.

The violin world is very fond of 'free-plate' tuning. The most common way of doing this is to excite the plate while it is suspended on foam blocks over a speaker which is fed by a sweepable signal generator that produces a sine wave from 100hz up to around 2Khz. Over this frequency range the plates will resonate in a number of predictable ways, though the fact the violin plates are not a regular shape, nor of uniform thickness does complicate matters.

The idea behind this is that if the soundboard and back of a good violin has its vibration modes at particular frequencies and the shape of those modes can be seen by exciting the plate with a fine material (sawdust, sand or glitter) scattered over it, another instrument can is made to vibrate in the same way at the same frequencies and it should sound just as good. Experience as well as trial and error is required to know how much wood to remove where, but that's the basic idea.

Guitar and bouzouki plates will resonate in the same way, but not as much experimental work has been done to correlate free plate modes with finished instruments. Partly this is because once the guitar or bouzouki plate is glued to the sides and a fingerboard glued over it, its behaviour changes and also for the very practical reason that it is much harder to get a guitar or bouzouki soundboard off once it is on compared to a violin to alter bracing or make other changes.

The more common way of measuring the response of a guitar or bouzouki is to excite the soundboard using the same sort of sweepable frequency generator mentioned before. This can be done with the instrument horizontal with a handheld speaker held just above the soundboard and dust or glitter used to show the modes as they appear.

A more complex approach involves physically driving the soundboard by means such as attaching a saddle to a loudspeaker voice coil or a magnet attached to the bridge driven by an oscillating magnetic field. By recording the sound radiated from the instrument and plotting frequency against amplitude (ie how loud it is), the vibrational modes of the soundboard, as well as the air resonance of soundbox itself can be accurately measured.

The diagram on the next page is the frequency responce of a 10 string instrument (using a low D string) built by my colleague Phill Kearney of Bundaberg, Queensland, which may be the first Irish bouzouki ever measured in this way.

While considerable experimental work has been done over the past forty years, first on violins and later on guitars, little has been done with Irish bouzoukis, though a lot of useful information can be extrapolated from information available on both violins and guitars. In essence, it boils down to a relationship between the note of the open bottom string of the instrument and the various frequencies at which the soundboard resonates. For example violin makers often want a violin soundboard to have a strong resonance between E and F# on the third (D) string. A bouzouki or cittern tuned an octave lower will also respond quite well if the soundboard resonates in those range of notes an octave lower though there are differences in the way the sound is generated and expectations of the sound produced.

Once the free-plate is glued to the sides the way the soundboard vibrates changes as the edges of the soundboard cannot move. The shape of the patterns themselves change and shift in frequency. Once the back is glued on the resonance of the enclosed volume of air is a factor, as that will resonate on a particular frequency, known as the Helmholtz Frequency or the air resonance. This is found by humming into the soundhole until a note is found which is much louder. On a good guitar this note is usually around G or G# on the bottom string, so this can be extrapolated to looking for an air resonance for a bouzouki around A# or B. On a guitar bodied instrument that is quite possible to achieve, but a smaller teardrop shaped instrument as described here will be more likely to have an air resonance around C or C# on the bottom string. If the resonance gets up to D, it will mean a very strong open D string, and the air resonance is preferably between two notes, so a frequency between C and C# is to be preferred. A shallower bodied instrument will have an even higher air resonance, though a smaller soundhole can offset that to some extent.

The experimental work done on guitars in the past few decades by such people as Graham Caldersmith, Al Carruth and others has shown that there should be a strong relationship between the air resonance and the first few soundboard resonance modes. The first vibrational mode of the soundboard, where the entire vibrating area of the board is moving as one, should occur close to an octave above the air resonance mentioned before. This is an indication of the basic stiffness of the soundboard, and if that note is too high, it affects the entire response of the instrument.

Having the air resonance higher than three or four frets above the open bottom string means the instrument won't have the richness in the bass, but that is not generally the intention of a bouzouki or cittern. As an instrument in a band it wants to have a distinctive tone separate from that of a guitar. If a bouzouki with the tonal range of a guitar for solo or accompanying work is wanted a body around a 00/classical size will work well.

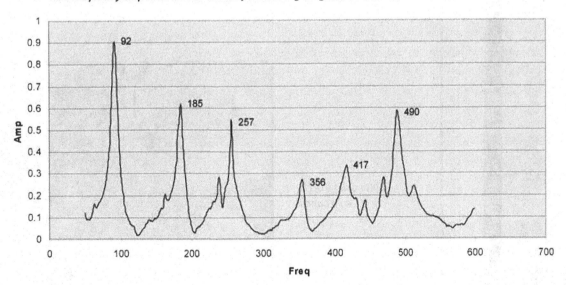

The frequency responce of Phill Kearney's 10-string long scale bouzouki

This chapter deals with two different approaches to making a heel-less neck. In this style of construction the neck is made first, and then the neck-block is made to accurately fit the neck.

For those who want a more traditional look with a heel that is described in the next chapter. That style of neck requires the soundboard to be attached to the sides, and uses a different syle of neck block with a vertical mortice matching a tenon on the neck and barrel nuts as the method to lock the neck and body together.

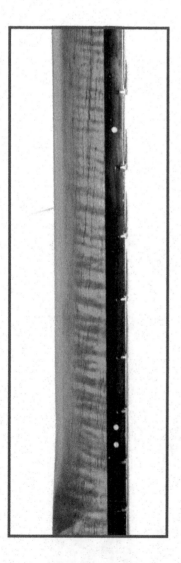

Background

For most of the history of fretted instruments it has been considered a necessity to have the body and neck as closely and permanently joined as possible. On classical guitars the usual way is the Spanish foot, where the heel of the neck itself becomes the gluing point for the sides, the soundboard and the back. On steel string guitars and mandolins it has usually been a glued dovetail joint which connects the neck to a separate wooden block in the body.

The reasoning behind this has always been that it allows the entire instrument to vibrate and resonate as one unit. and there is certainly evidence from the violin world that the resonances of the neck, the fingerboard and tailpiece have noticeable effects on the overall sound of the instrument, though I don't know of similar work that has been done on fretted instruments.

The disadvantage is that when it becomes a necessity for maintenance or repair work to be done to the neck or fingerboard, having that neck or fingerboard firmly fixed to the body makes it a lot harder.

Frets wear out and have to be replaced' necks occasionally bend and twist in unexpected ways and any slight movement or rotation in the area of the neck block can mean the neck pulling upwards and the instrument becoming much harder to play than it should be. Specialised techniques and tools have been developed over the past twenty or thirty years to remove dovetailed necks and to assist with hammering in frets into the area of the fingerboard over the soundboard.

The answer, I became convinced over some years, was to make the neck removable, and to be able to construct the neck and its mounting in the body using the tools I had and jigs I could make with them. I was always impressed by Steve Klein's horizontal dovetail, but it seemed a little more complicated than I wanted to do. Robert Cumpiano's pinned mortice and tenon was the next inspiration, and I adapted that to use barrel nuts in the tenon and matching bolts that I found I could buy from the hardware store as things to assemble knockdown furniture. It wasn't until I had built a few that I discovered Taylor guitars used a similar system, and that bolt-on necks were quite widely used. The disadvantage of living on the far side of the world!

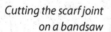
Cutting the scarf joint on a bandsaw

The barrel nut method certainly simplified getting the neck off for any necessary work, but still used a heel which had to be carefully fitted to the body to achieve the correct neck angle and an extension to the neck to support the fingerboard over the body. I have always favoured fretting the fingerboard after it has been glued to the neck, and I wanted a way that would make the fretting process (and eventual refretting) as simple as possible.

To my mind the obvious answer was making necks in a similar way to the one Leo Fender worked out over fifty years ago. Fender built acoustic guitars in the 60s using their electric style necks and very long wood screws going through a large and heavy neck block. While wood screws are fine going into a heavy and tight grained timber like Rock Maple I am less comfortable using them on timbers like Mahogany or Australian Blackwood, especially when there is the expectation that they might well be removed and replaced a number of times.

As an alternative I decided to use T-nuts inserted in the neck under the fingerboard. I use 1/4" steel units which take a common 1/4" USC or BSW or metric M6 threaded machine bolt. Smaller types like 3/16" or those using a 10-32 thread (commonly used for holding speakers in speaker cabinets) could be used. It is a matter of what can be found easily.

The finished neck is mounted on the body in a mortice routed into a hollow head block (see Chapter 7 on Sides & Blocks) and fixed with machine bolts inserted through the soundhole into the hollow headblock.

The two heel-less necks use many of the same techniques, the main difference being the basic structure. The first of these uses one piece of 75x25mm (3x1") quartersawn timber with the headstock cut off and attached with a glued scarf joint. The second laminates two or more pieces of timber from which the neck is then cut out in one piece. For the first type well quartered and straight timber is necessary. For the laminated version the direction of the annular rings is not important as the two (or even three) pieces are glued bookmatched so any tendency of the timber to move is balanced out.

It is still important for the grain of the timber to run as straight as possible along the length of the neck for strength and stability.

Of course if a suitable piece of well quartered wood can be found from which the whole neck profile can be cut out in one piece this can be used. But remember, you can get two scarf jointed necks from the same piece of wood, and they will probably be stronger. Any neck cut from one piece of wood has a weak point where the neck itself joins the head, as the grain of the wood which should run along the length of the neck will run across the angled head. Ask any guitar repairer how many headstocks they have repaired.

No neck building technique is perfect. The angled headstock will always be a weak point, especially with 8 or 10 machine heads attached to it and the considerable pull of the strings adding to its inherent fragility, but all three of these building techniques minimise the chance of a break. You can also do things like insert carbon graphite bars into the neck which can overlap at the head join to strengthen it.

Planing the scarf joint

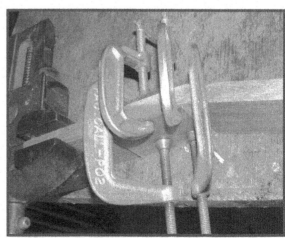

Gluing the scarf joint

All these neck types utilise a doubled over truss rod which is a little over 10mm deep. It has been suggested that neck rods work better the deeper they are set into the neck, so I set the rods into a slot cut 12mm deep in the neck blank, and glue in a fillet of wood, which is then trimmed down, into the slot over the rod. Apart from the mechanical advantage of the deeper set rod, gluing on the fillet over the rod means the rod is well seated in the bottom of the slot, and that the pressure of rod adjustment is evenly distributed along the neck.

One advantage of the laminated neck is that extra timber can be left in the area under the nut in the style of some of the early Martin guitars if you want to adjust the rod from the head end. Making a neck in this way has always had the disadvantage of the 'straight' grain on the neck itself, becoming 'short' grain in the angled headstock, and once you also route out a groove that allows access to the rod adjustment nut there is not much timber left to hold the headstock onto the neck. A peak or 'volute' on the back of the neck under this weak spot minimised the chance of a broken head. .

I suggest this for an arched-top instrument as the end of the neck being raised above the soundboard will make accessing the truss rod nut without removing the neck difficult

Alternatively, if the scarf joint neck is used it is suggested that the adjustment nut is placed at the body end of the neck. With a flat soundboard access can be made through the soundhole, with an appropriately sized hole being drilled horizontally through the end of the neck mortice. It is still quite practical to access the nut through the head end on a scarf joint neck if you want to make such a neck for an arch-top.

Scarf Joint Neck

Select a piece of appropriate wood (as listed in the Materials section) 25mm x 75mm x 850mm (1x3x33"), and plane or machine it down to 20mm x 72mm. (The exact thickness and width is not really important, but don't machine it any thinner than 18mm (3/4") or narrower than 70mm) A perfect bit of wood will have the grain running exactly parallel to the wide surface, but it is rarely a perfect world. If it doesn't, it is preferable for any runout to be angled towards the nut (picture). This is because you will be planing the flat surface towards the nut position, and this will minimise tearout. Mark the top (fingerboard) surface and the head end.

Measure 200mm (8") from the nut end, and mark it on the side of the neck blank. From the top of the neck at that point draw a 15° line back towards the head end. Saw off this end piece with a tenon saw or on the bandsaw.

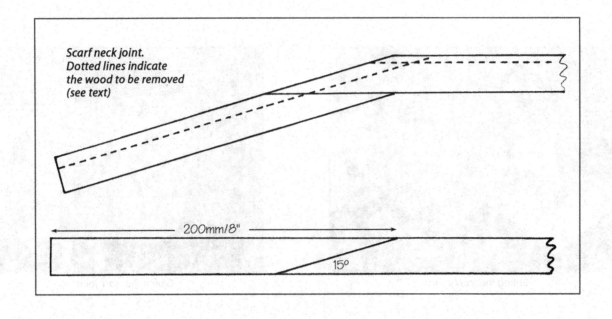

Scarf neck joint.
Dotted lines indicate
the wood to be removed
(see text)

200mm/8"

15º

Clamp the large piece to the workbench with the off cut on top so the two angled surfaces line up. Plane and sand this exactly flat. A well set up plane set for a very fine cut should be able to achieve the necessary accuracy, but a small sanding block can also be useful. The angled surface on the off cut is glued to the bottom of the large piece and this is a critical glue joint. With a small straightedge check for flatness both along and across the angled face. A light sand of the gluing area of the longer piece might be useful to clean that up and remove any machine marks, but make sure that it is flat as well, and not curved by the sanding.

Clamp the short piece firmly to the workbench on its side (I use a Versa-Vice in the horizontal position). Apply glue to the angled face and locate the longer piece in position and hold lightly with a clamp. Use 3mm perspex cauls on either side of the gluing area and clamp lightly. Tighten up the clamps on the longer piece to firmly hold that in position, and then tighten up the clamps over the glue joint. It is important to keep the sides of the two pieces firmly on the workbench to maintain alignment of the two sections. This will make it easier when it comes to marking out centrelines and routing the truss-rod slot. A small piece of cling wrap under the gluing area will stop glue ooze sticking the neck to the workbench, but be careful not to catch the clingwrap in the glue joint. Let dry overnight.

The next step is to reduce the neck blank to the correct thickness. The head should have a finished thickness of 15mm (5/8") with the veneer overlay, so the 20mm thick blank needs to be reduced to 15mm less whatever veneer you are using. I usually use a 2mm dark timber (ebony or rosewood) backed with a light (maple or similar) standard thickness veneer, but that is optional. The 2mm overlay has the advantage of adding strength to the scarf joint, and combined with the thinner pale veneer gives a good definition to the head shape. This means reducing the head thickness to around 12.5mm (1/2"), and the amount to be removed is marked with a pencil on all three sides of the head. Remember you want to remove the wood from the top of the head, not the back. The excess can either be planed away or bandsawn off the top surface leaving 1mm to be planed and sanded. A fence on the bandsaw is useful to keep the surface vertical.

The neck must now be reduced in thickness, to 16mm at the nut increasing to 18mm at the end of the neck. The neck blank will be too long at this point, and should be cut to length. Allow 5mm at the head end for the nut, measure along the neck to the position where the neck joins the body, and then add the distance the neck is set into the body (70mm or as much as you have determined with your own design). Cut the neck blank to length, allowing 5mm extra for final trimming. Planing the top surface of the neck down will shift the nut position towards the head a few mm in any case so there will be some leeway.

Measure up from the bottom of the neck (16mm at the nut and 18mm at the end of the neck) and pencil a line on both sides. Clamp the neck in a vice and plane down to just above the lines. Finish off with a large sanding block to get this entire surface as flat as possible in both dimensions if you can't achieve this with the plane alone. Check with a straight edge in all directions. Make sure you haven't planed or sanded in a twist. Check for this by sighting down the length of the upper surface with two 150mm (6") long sticks place across the width of the neck, one at each end. The next step is making a truss-rod and routing out a slot for it. A flat surface on the neck surface is essential for a flat slot for the rod, as well as a flat surface to glue on the fingerboard.

The Laminated Neck

For this style of neck you will need either a piece of 125x50mm (5"x2") timber from which the two laminates can be cut or one long piece of 50x65mm (2"x2 1/2") wood - twice the length of the neck you want to make. Quartersawn timber is not essential for this style of neck, but straight grain along the length is still important. Try to select a piece with consistent annular rings along the length of it by looking at each end of the wood. If using one longer piece cut it in half. If you don't have a good and well set-up planer and thicknesser, find a local woodworker who does, and have the piece(s) of timber machined straight and square. Exact dimensions don't matter, but try not to lose too much. You want 75mm (3") total with and at least 50mm (2") or more depth in the finished blank.

Possible end grain on a laminated neck

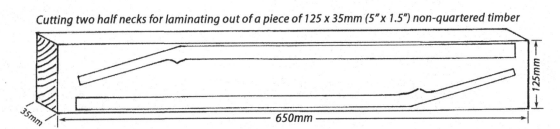
Cutting two half necks for laminating out of a piece of 125 x 35mm (5" x 1.5") non-quartered timber

Work out how the two piece of wood are going to be aligned when glued so the annular rings at each end are bookmatched. Also keep in mind if the grain isn't exactly along the line of the neck to have the runout going in the same direction. Mark the edges that will be joined with a pencil so that when you are gluing you know what gets glued to what.

Glue the two pieces together. Don't worry about getting the alignment exact, but a couple of 6mm dowels in opposite corners that will be cut away later helps stop any tendency for the wood to slide around. Don't use too much glue, though you should have a little squeezeout on each side once clamped.

Leave for 24 hours and remove the clamps. Plane and sand the fingerboard surface flat and straight. This will be the reference surface for everything else you do to the neck blank, so get this right. The glue joint in the middle of this surface will remain the centreline of the neck. The fingerboard surface also needs to be at 90° to at least one side of the laminated blank, with the centreline parallel to that side. This will allow you to accurately bandsaw the neck profile and route the truss-rod slot.

On one side of the laminated blank mark out the head. If the blank has only one side at 90° to the fingerboard surface, do your marking on the other. Allow 200mm (8") from one end, and draw a line at a 15° angle from the nut position. This establishes the top surface of the head, excluding the veneers, which will be glued on later.

Draw another line 12-13mm below that to establish the back of the head. Allow another 5mm (3/16") from the point where the head joins the neck for the nut and then mark out the 12th fret position, the position of whichever fret occurs at the body join, and the remainder of the neck extension into the body. Using a square, make a pencil mark 16mm below the top surface of the neck at the nut and other 18mm below the top surface at the end of the neck. Join these two lines and draw in the volute to finish the neck profile.

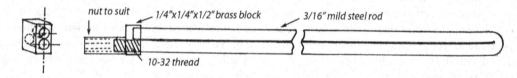

Cutting the 10-32 thread labels: nut to suit · 1/4"x1/4"x1/2" brass block · 3/16" mild steel rod · 10-32 thread

Cutting the 10-32 thread

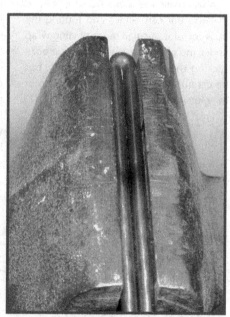

Bending the rod in the vice

Cut off the excess wood from the top of the head, and plane and sand the top surface of the head, making sure you don't go past the line marking the nut position. If using a router table to cut the trussrod slot, the neck profile can be cut out at this point. If using a a handheld router with a fence leave cutting out the neck profile until after the rod is fitted, as the bulk of the laminated block will make it easier to hold it in a vice while routing.

The Trussrod

The trussrod is made from a length of 3/16" mild steel rod. The diagram shows its basic construction. For the scarf-joint neck I suggest that the rod be adjusted from the neck end. For a laminated neck with a volute the adjustment can be from the head end, which is often more convenient.

The most common thread used is a 3/16" 10-32 UNF, which both Fender and Gibson use, and there are a variety of nuts available, such as the Fender bullet type, the Gibson brass hexagonal and the allen key style. I recommend the allen key type, though all work well. Luthiers Mercantile International (LMI) sell one which is only 1/4" in outside diameter, which minimises the amount of wood that has to be removed.

Both Luthiers Mercantile and Stewart-McDonald sell various sized trussrods which may fit your neck.

Start with a 1m (39") length of rod. Wipe the rod down with some paper towelling dampened with acetone to remove any grease or oil. Square off one end on a disk sander or grinding wheel and put a small bevel around the edge. Clamp the rod in a vice with around 50mm (2") protruding. With a 3/16" 10-32 die in a holder start winding the cutter onto the rod. For the first cut tighten the adjusting grub screw on the die holder to expand the die to its maximum diameter. A light oil on the die will help. You will probably get a revolution or so before the teeth start to bite. As it starts to bite into the rod, stop and back off a little and you will feel a 'click' as the kerf is broken off. Advance the cutter another third of a revolution or so and back off a little until the click breaks off the next bit of kerf and continue until there is about 20mm of thread. Remove the die and check the fit of the nut. With the die adjusted to it's maximum diameter the nut will be a little too tight on the thread, so back off the adjusting grub screws a little and re-cut the thread a little narrower. This will clean up any rough bits of the thread from the first cut.

Thread a nut onto the rod about 6-7mm and lay it on top of the neck so the nut is positioned in the correct place. For a head adjusting rod, the brass block should sit under the bone string nut. For adjustment from the body end of the neck the adjusting nut should end 5mm short of the end of the neck itself (which should be 70mm from the fret marking the body join) and stop at the nutend of the fretboard. Mark the place on the rod where it has to bend with chalk or a wax pencil.

Using a propane torch (or oxyacetylene) heat the rod at the marked position until red hot and then bend the rod back 180° and then squash in a vice as quickly as possible. It will probably be necessary to reheat the rod to red-heat and re-squash it in the vice to get the bend tight so that the two lengths sit neatly on top of one another, especially around the bend.

On a length of 1/4" square brass rod draw a centreline on one side and mark off a point 7/32" from one end and another 3/16" further on. Drill 3/16" holes at both point, which should mean that the edges of the holes just touch. One hole should be drilled all the way through the rod and the other halfway through. Cut the piece off with a hacksaw 1/16" (1.5mm) past the second hole and clean up the ends with a file or the disk sander.

The brass bearing block

Routing the trussrod slot

Clamp the bent over length of steel rod in the vice and cut the non-threaded end off so around 6mm (1/4") (back to metric) would extend through the hole in the brass rod and the cut-off end would sit in the blind hole. It is useful to file a bevel on the non-threaded end. Fit the brass block onto the rod and slide a length of shrink wrap tubing over the steel rod, but keep it away from the thread at the end. Heat it with a hot air gun or the propane torch so it is tight over the rod and the two parts of the rod are tightly together. Thread on the nut and the trussrod is ready.

Fitting the trussrod

The trussrod will be slightly over 3/16" (5mm) in width and slightly more than 3/8" (10mm) in height, due to the wrapping around the rod. Specially sized and round-ended router bits are available, but a 3/16" or 5mm bit will work fine to route out the slot. The slot will be 12mm deep to allow a spline to be fitted on top to assure a tight vertical fit of the trussrod. This is essential for it to work properly. A router table is best, but a hand-held router with an edge guide will work as well with the blank held firmly in a vice.

On the fingerboard surface of the blank draw two lines 3/16" or 5mm apart centred on the middle of the neck. On the body end of the neck extend these two lines vertically down 12mm so you know how deep to route. If you are using a head-end adjustment you will rout the slot right though the blank from end to end. For a body-end adjustment you will want to stop the slot just before the nut. If you are using a router table make a mark on the fence where the end of the neck has to come to or clamp a block of scrap wood to the router table to stop the neck going to far.

The finished slot needs to be slightly wider than the router bit, so line up the cutting edge of the bit with the outside of one of the two vertical lines on the end of the neck, and tighten up the table fence or edge guide. Don't try to route a 12mm deep slot all at once, do it in 2-3mm increments, keeping the area where the fence meets the table clean of dust and shreds of wood. Remember routers are dangerous things, and having the bit grab the neck blank and fling it around the workshop is going to be dangerous to you, and won't do the neck any good either.

Once the slot is 12mm deep check the fit of the trussrod. It is likely that it won't fit, so the fence or edge guide will need to be adjusted just a fraction - like .5mm or a little more than 1/64" to widen it. Check how the slot is in relation to the centreline and adjust accordingly. Route out that bit extra from one side and check the fit of the rod again. Repeat if necessary until the rod just slips into the slot with gentle pressure.

The brass block at the adjustment end of the rod, and the adjustment nut itself are wider than the rod, so the appropriate end of the slot must be widened. The brass block should be 1/4" (6.25mm) wide and extend a mm or so above and below the rod itself. The allen key nut needs just enough clearance around it so it won't jam on the wood, so the slot can either be enlarged by the router or with a chisel. The rod needs to sit firmly on the bottom of the slot without being lifted off by the brass block sitting too high.

Prepare a capping piece for the rod out of the same wood the neck is made of, preferably from the same piece. Using the same wood minimises the possibly of different amounts of movement through humidity changes.

Measuring the angle of the head

Sanding the nut end of the head overlay to match the angle

The capping piece needs to fit as closely as possible in the top couple of millimetres of the slot, so it needs to be planed to the exact width of the slot and around 4mm deep. If it does get a bit narrower in spots don't worry too much, as it will be held firmly in place by the fingerboard, but you do want to be able to glue it in place.

Run a bead of glue along each side of the top of the slot and glue in the capping piece with a strip of wood or MDF as a caul on top. Leave overnight and then plane and sand the capping strip flush with the top surface of the neck.

If making a laminated neck and the neck profile hasn't yet been cut out, do it at this point, leaving an extra millimetre or so thickness along the length of the neck and head. The head thickness should have been calculated at 15mm less whatever overlay and/or veneers you wanted to use. The section of the neck that will fit into the body mortice should be planed to 18mm (3/4") thick and of course parallel to the top surface. You can also taper the bottom of the neck from 18mm at the body join to 16mm at the 1st fret position at this point, but it isn't necessary.

The Head Overlay

The finished thickness of the head should be between 14-15mm, though it can look interesting to have the thickness of the head taper towards the end. Any less than 14mm, where a machine head is mounted, does run the risk of not being able to tighten the top nut to clamp the machine head in place, though this is not so important with press-fit ferrules. Nevertheless buy the machine heads first and check the minimum head thickness required. Trim down the overlay to the width of the head on the neck, allowing a little extra length. With a sliding bevel and a square work out the head angle and set the disc sander table to that angle. From one side of the overlay mark a square line and sand in that angle on the end that to the back of the nut. The end of the overlay should then be square to the neck surface.

Clamp a small machinist's square to the neck surface right at the break angle, and clamp the overlay on the head surface so it sits tightly against the square. Drill 2 x 1/16" inch holes in opposite corners (where they will be trimmed away) and push in two 1/16" pins.

Cut out a clamping caul from a piece of perspex or 12mm plywood and drill a couple of matching (but somewhat larger) holes to clear the pins. Remove the overlay and if using rosewood wipe down the gluing surface with acetone. This will remove the surface oils which could cause later failure of the glue joint. Apply a thin coat of glue over the head surface, smoothing it over with a piece of scrap veneer or similar. Get the pins back in place to locate the overlay and clamp it all together. Remove the machinist's square and wipe away the squeezeout, especially at the nut end.

Leave this to dry overnight, as the glued surface will take a while to dry completely. Mark and cut out your head shape, leaving a little excess and sand or plane this down to its final shape. Mark the position of the machine heads. I have a 25mm long flare from the nut to the head's widest point, and then allow another 15mm until the first post. The centre points for the posts are 10mm in from the edge and 27mm apart using small button machine heads.

Drilling the machine head holes

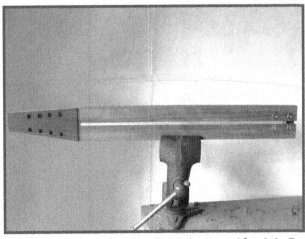

A neck ready for the fingerboard with the trussrod fitted, the T-nuts installed and the head shaped

Using machine heads with large buttons would need more distance between them (guitars are typically use 37mm (1.5") spacing). Check how much clearance is needed before drilling the holes. It is no fun trying to fill in and hide holes drilled in the wrong place. A 10mm spur or doweling bit will minimise tearout when drilling. Drill from the back of the head with the face backed by a piece of scrap MDF.

If four-on-a-plate mandolin heads are to be used, measure the post spacing and the clearance necessary for the end of the plate on the neck end. It looks bad to have the mounting plate protrude into the flare of the head. Good quality mandolin heads such as Schaller use a 6mm post, but the bushing that is press-fitted into the overlay side is tapered from 10mm wide at the top. Either drill an 8mm (5/16") hole and ream it out with a peg reamer or drill a 3/8" (which is about 9.5mm) hole and file a small taper into it. In either case the bushing will want to be a tight press fit. The final adjustment of the bushing holes can be left until fitting the machine heads as the holes tend to get a little smaller from grain filler and lacquer.

If making a laminated neck, with the truss rod adjustment at the head end, the same bit can be used to drill away the overlay over the rod's nut. Leave 6mm or so closest to the nut and carefully drill through the overlay, and then clean up with a chisel and a 10mm round file.

Reduce the thickness of the laminated headstock to 15mm by removing wood from the back. A Wagner Safe-T-Planer is quick and effective, otherwise a block plane and chisels. Only go to the end of the volute with the Safe-T-Planer and leave the rest until final carving of the neck

The Fingerboard

At the initial design stage you will have determined the scale length of your instrument.   Appendix 3 lists the fret positions for both a 22" (560mm) and a 26" (660mm) scale, with the formula for calculating other scales. These are in metric as this is the easiest way to mark out the fingerboard.

Fingerboards are usually ebony or rosewood, but other hard, dense woods are sometimes used. Lutherie suppliers can sell you thicknessed and pre-slotted fingerboards, or you can start off with a rough sawn blank and do it all yourself. With a blank, the first thing to do is reduce it in thickness to 1/4" (6.25mm). This can be done by hand with a plane and a simple a simple shooting board . The plane needs to be as sharp as possible, as both rosewood and ebony will take the edge off a plane blade very quickly. Alternatively a thickness sanding machine or a blade thicknesser will do the job quickly and accurately.

Once the blank is reduced to just a little more than 1/4", finish off with the half sheet sanding board. The bottom face of the blank should be as flat as possible for gluing to the neck. Square off one edge, either with a buzzer or a long plane on a shooting board. This edge has to be straight as a reference for cutting the fret slots.

Planing the fingerboard profile

Positioning the fingerboard

With a long ruler clamped to the fingerboard mark off the fret positions with a sharp scribe or bradawl. These want to be within 1/10mm to get the frets in the right positions. Using a small machinist's square and a scribing tool mark off right across the fingerboard the lines for the fret slots. Remember that the distance from the nut to the first fret needs to be half the saw kerf (~ .012"/.3mm) further towards the head end of the fingerboard so sit the nut in the correct position.
.

With a fretting saw (a narrow .023" kerf backsaw) and the square held firmly against the straight edge cut slots 2.5-3mm deep in all the fret positions you want. This will be easier to do if the fingerboard is firmly clamped to the work bench. Cut right through the fingerboard at the nut position.

Mark the centreline of the fingerboard about 30mm in from the straight edge. A four course fingerboard will be 34mm wide at the nut and 44mm wide at the 12th fret. A five course (with an extra high string) will be 42mm wide at the nut and 54mm wide at the 12th fret. Draw pencil lines joining the nut and 12th fret positions to establish the fretboard width. Make sure the centreline position allows enough width at the end of the fingerboard. If not mark another centreline and redraw the edge lines.

Cut out the fingerboard on the bandsaw leaving a millimetre or so clear of the pencilled edges. On the shooting board trim down the fingerboard to its exact size with a plane. If you wish to have a couple of extra frets past the end of the neck the end of the board can be trimmed and shaped to suit at this point. A fingerboard extension can be useful to hide the joins of your soundhole rosette.

Powered alternative

A small table saw can be fitted with a narrow kerfed 6" fret slotting blade. A jig such as in the picture can be made of a stable timber, in this case rock maple. The slotting jigs can be purchased from suppliers like Stewart McDonald, or custom made by someone with a computer controlled overhead router. Sign makers and/or perspex fabricators often have such machinery and if you give them the exact measurements it is a simple job for them to do. The locating slots in this jig are exactly 1/8" wide and the pin in the large wooden block is a broken off 1/8" drill bit positioned so a 1/4" thick fingerboard blank with the slotting jig attached lines up with the pin. The slotting jigs are held onto the fretboard blank with double sided tape.

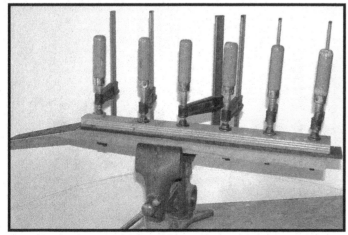

Gluing the fingerboard

A table saw set up with a fret slotting template

Installing the T-nuts

Trim the neck to its exact length, which will give you 70mm of neck extending into the body. In the same way the fingerboard width was laid out, draw the fingerboard edges on the neck surface, marking the 12th fret and the fret that occurs at the body join. Four t-nuts are used to attach the neck to the body and these are fitted to the neck underneath the fingerboard. The size doesn't really matter, as long as you have the space to fit the round top of the t-nuts between the trussrod and the edge of the neck, preferably leaving a couple of millimetres on the outside.

Mark the centre positions of the t-nuts as indicated on the neck block diagram in the fold-out plans at the back of the book. With a forstner bit drill out shallow holes 1mm deeper than the top of the t-nuts, and then holes to clear the barrels of the t-nuts. Tap them in lightly with a hammer and push them all the way in with a bolt threaded in and squeezed in the vice.

Cut out circles of thin card the same size as the top of the t-nuts and superglue them to the tops of each one. This is why the shallow holes were drilled deeper than the thickness of the t-nuts and it stops glue from the fingerboard gluing leaking in the t-nut thread.

Gluing the fingerboard

Clamp the fingerboard in position on the neck and with a 1/16" bit drill through the 1st fret slot (off to one side of the trussrod) about 3mm into the neck. Do the same with a fret slot up near the body join (though not over one of the t-nuts). Tap 1/16" pins into each hole.

Make clamping caul just a little smaller than the fingerboard and drill clearance holes in the same place as the pins. This can be simply a piece of 12-16mm MDF with 6mm x 2mm strips of scrap timber glued along the edges. Remove the fingerboard and if using rosewood wipe the gluing surface with acetone several times and let dry (which will only take a few seconds) Coat the underside of the fingerboard thinly and evenly with glue, locate it on the neck with the pins and clamp it with several clamps.

If there are a few of the higher frets past the end of the neck, make sure there is no glue on that part of the underneath of the fingerboard and remove the glue squeezeout along the sides of the board and especially at the nut position. A narrow strip of card or a large plastic drinking straw cut at an angle works well for this.

Leave this to dry overnight and remove the clamps. Cut the neck close to final to width on the bandsaw, but be careful not to cut intothe fingerboard. At the same time cut out the flared section of the headstock.

A router table it can be used to trim the width exactly using a ball bearing bit. A 1/2" diameter/ 1" long bit with the same size ball bearing is fitted to the router with the bearing level with the table and the bit protruding above. The neck is placed fingerboard side down and the bearing rides along the edge of the fingerboard and trims the neck square. Be careful to feed the neck into the rotation of the bit, and keep your fingers away.

Shaping the Fingerboard and Fretting

A lot has been written about fretboard radii with adherents to one continuous radius up the length of the fretboard and others who argue for a conical section where the radius of the board gets progressively greater the further up up the board. There are a number of tools and jigs that can be bought to achieve this. This is a simpler method which gives the board an approximately conical section. The critical factor is getting the fingerboard flat along its length.

Sanding the fingerboard arch

For a four course neck mark a line 1mm down from the top of the board along each side or 1.5mm (1/16") for a five course neck. With a sharp plane set shallow plane away the side of the board down to the line along a strip 6-8mm wide so it looks

1st facet   2nd facet

like this (somewhat exaggerated):
Plane another facet leaving a 6-8mm strip in the middle untouched.

With a long sanding block (the length of a sheet of sandpaper and 75mm - 3" or more wide) faced with 80 grit paper turn those five facets into a smooth curve. Check with a 300mm (1 ft) straight edge along the length. Once you have got the curve smooth and flat along the length repeat with a block faced with 120 grit.

It is usual to inlay fret markers on the top of the fingerboard. These can be as simple as 1/16" white plastic dots (using the plastic rod used for the position markers on the sides of the fingerboard), or mother-of pearl dots or anything else you fancy.

Lutherie suppliers will have a range of pre-cut dots, snowflakes and diamonds as well as blank pieces of various kinds of shell for your own designs.

Inlays of contrasting wooden veneers or metal are also used. A look around your local guitar shop will give lots of ideas, but simpler is often better. Markers are commonly inserted at the 3rd, 5th, 7th and 12th frets, and sometimes at the 9th or 10th and the 15th. The 12th fret markers are often a little larger, or two are used.

If using Mother of Pearl (MOP) dots it is a simple matter of drilling a hole in the centre of the fingerboard slightly shallower than the dot and supergluing it in. The 3rd fret position marker is placed halfway between the 2nd and 3rd frets and so forth. With the 120 grit sanding board sand the dots flush with the board and continue sanding with 180 grit, 240 grit and 360 or 400 grit, being careful not to make the board thinner at the nut end.

It is not unknown for the plane to tear out a little at the fret slot edges or if the grain of the fingerboard changes direction. After the 120 grit sanding, clean all the dust away and check for tearouts. Fill with a drop of superglue and some of the dust and sand flat again. Repeat if necessary.

Check the depth of the fret slots at the sides and deepen a little if necessary. In any case clean out the slots with the fretsaw.

Between 900-1200mm (3-4ft) of fretwire will be needed. I use a standard 2mm wire but you could use a narrow banjo/ mandolin wire or wider jumbo guitar wire. Some wire comes in a roll, which is handy because you don't have to bend it into a curve to use it. Other manufacturers supply it as straight strips, which means that it has to be pre-bent into a curve before hammering it into place. You can buy a fretwire curling machine, but it can be easily done with a pair of ground down endnippers. You can either cut the fretwire to length for each fret, allowing a couple of mm overhang at each end or tap it in straight off the roll or strip and cut each piece off after hammering it into place.

Fingerboard position markers

Installing frets

The fret wire can be hammered into place using either a dedicated fretting hammer, or as I use, an old ballpeen hammer that I inherited from my father-in-law. Tap in each end, keeping the tang vertical and work across the fret. It can be useful to run a thin bead of white PVA or animal glue into the slot before tapping the fret into place, but remember to wipe off the squish-out with a damp rag after each fret. The essential thing is to make sure the frets are seated evenly across the fretboard, so the tops of them are as even as possible.

Once all the frets are in place cut the ends off with the endnippers, and run a file along the sides of the fretboard to smooth it off. I use a medium cut file about 300mm (1 ft) long which is also good for the final fret levelling. Once the edges are smooth file a bevel along the ends of the frets at around a 60° angle from the fretboard. You can buy a special tool to do this, but the angle isn't critical and it only takes a couple of minutes to do.

Shaping the neck

This style of heel-less neck makes carving the neck profile a simpler operation than having to deal with a heel. The idea is to remove successive facets from the rectangular neck to create the finished neck. Below are suggested cross-sections for four- and five-course necks with the first tangents drawn in. Draw lines on the sides and bottom of the neck connecting the points at the 1st and 12th fret positions where the tangents cross the rectangular shape. Draw a line around the neck at whatever fret position marks the neck/body join. With a chisel or drawknife remove that outside triangular section from each side, making sure you don't remove any wood from the area that remains square inside the body mortice. You need to carve a smooth curve joining the section inside the body to the neck profile in a similar way that the headstock joins the neck

Once the first facet is carved take away two more smaller facets on either side, overlapping the edges of the first facet. The new top facet should almost overlap the bottom edge of the fingerboard.

Continue to remove another smaller facet over each joining point and the neck should be approaching a final shape. From here on it is 80 grit sandpaper and scrapers to achieve the final shape. The curve of the neck's cross section should start around 2.5mm from the top edge of the fingerboard. This allows a slight bevel on the top edge of the fingerboard which just takes the edges of the frets a little away from the fingers

A subtle but important part of neck shaping is that at any point around the curvature of the neck there should be a straight line along the neck from the point where the curve from the square-edged neck extension becomes the neck profile to under the nut. A cross section should change quite quickly from the rectangular section to the carved neck profile - usually within 20mm or so. A good way to check this is is to rotate the neck in front of you and look tangentially across it. It is all to common to see necks which get rather bulbous towards the ends. This is a factor to keep in mind especially when carving a neck with a heel.

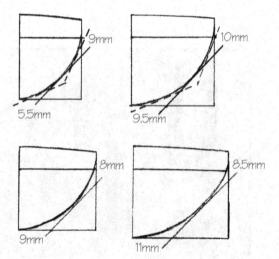

Cross section of an 8 string neck and (below) a 10 string neck with measurements for marking the the first facet to be removed. Both are measured at the 1st and 12th frets. The dotted lines on the upper diagram indicate the second round of faceting.
Note that the curve of the neck shaft starts halfway down the side of the fingerboard

The area where the headstock becomes the neck is also where a square section changes into the curved neck profile. The top edge of the flared section should remain vertical but should then fair into the curve of the neck, and the point in the centre of the the neck where the scarf joint joins the main section should be the place where the two shapes flow into each other.

If you chose to make a laminated neck with a volute the carving of this are is a little more complicated. The flat underside of the headstock should continue along the sides of the volute, and blend into the point from all directions. 80 grit sandpaper wrapped around a length of 25mm dowel as used on the workboard is good to clean up the shape.

Once the neck shape has been established with 80 grit paper, repeat with 120 and 180 grit making sure all the scratches from the 80 grit are removed. A final going over with 240 or 280 grit paper will have it ready for finishing and you may admire your work.

Marking the neck carving facets

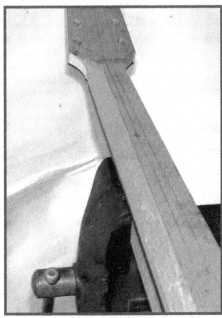

The first facet carved

The neck shaped before final sanding

While the basic structure of the heeled neck can be made at any time, the soundboard (of whatever kind) must be glued to the side assembly before the neck can be fitted to the correct angle. The neck is attached by two barrel nuts set horizontally in a vertical tenon which matches a mortice cut in the neckblock, with two long bolts pulling the neck onto the body.

In many ways the information in this chapter needs to be considered with the instructions in Chapter 7 which deals with constructing the side and block assembly.

A neck with a heel can be built either with with a scarf jointed head and a vertically laminated heel in the style of many Spanish classical guitars or a 2 or more piece side-by-side lamination. The height of the laminated block will need to be at least 90mm. At least one side of the heel section needs to be square to the top surface to allow the necessary routing to take place.

The neck needs to be 25mm longer than the measured distance from the nut to the fret where the body joins the neck, the extra 25mm being for the 20mm tenon that takes the barrel nuts with a little excess to trim away. The heel block should be 50-60mm long.

The processes for constructing the head and installing the trussrod are the same as a heel-less neck. For an archtop instrument the rod will need to be adjusted though the head end of the neck and stop short of the tenon.

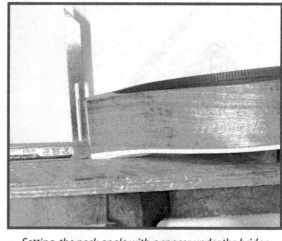

Setting the neck angle with a spacer under the bridge position

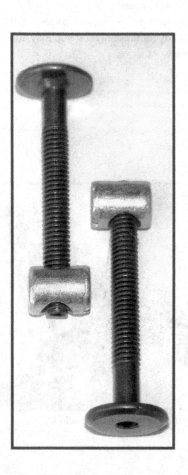

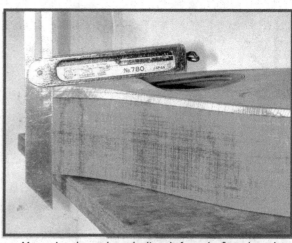

Measuring the neck angle directly from the fingerboard support

For a flat-top instrument there is the option of drilling through the head block and having the adjustment through the soundhole, but it will need a 50mm (2") long hole drilled lengthways through the block.

The first thing to do is to establish the neck angle. With a flat soundboard it should be close to 90°, but check anyway. With an arched soundboard the neck will be tilted back around 7°, but this needs to be an exact measurement.

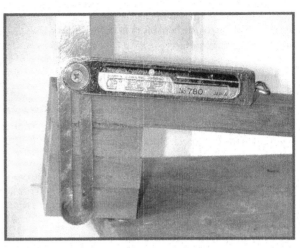

Transfering the angle to the end of the neck

Make up a support for the soundboard so that when placed face down on a workboard it follows the curvature of the soundboard across the soundboard at the bridge position. It should be 10mm in the middle and support the body so the sides are vertical and the edges are the same distance from the workboard. Place a piece of 5mm wood at the neck end of the soundboard. The 5mm block is to allow for the 5mm over-standing of the neck above the soundboard, but this can be varied if you wish. Use a sliding bevel to measure the angle from the workboard to the front of the body and transfer this to the neck heel block.

Drilling 7mm holes for the neck attachment bolts

If making a moulded archtop with the extra lamination, the top surface of the lamination will need to be planed to the correct angle before fitting the neck. This should be done in a plane that would end 10mm above the soundboard at the bridge and 3-5mm above the height of the binding. The sliding bevel can then measure the angle between that surface and the end of the body.

Draw lines at this angle at both the body join position and 20mm past it. Cut the excess off the end of the neck and sand flat to the line on a disc sander, indexing off the side of the neck block you know is square to the fingerboard surface. Estimate the total required height of the heel - ie body depth or body depth plus over-standing - and mark this down the angled end surface of the neck.

Drilling 10mm holes for the barrel nuts

Sand the bottom of the heel block at right angles to the back surface.

On the top surface of the neck mark the fingerboard width along the whole length of the neck as well as the 20mm width of the tenon to fit in the mortice that that has been cut in the body neck block. The 7mm holes in the neck block need duplicated in the heel block and drilled perpendicular to the back of the block. When measuring for these holes take into consideration the thickness of the soundboard at the end of the body and any neck over-stand.

These holes are in turn matched up to 10mm holes drilled sideways through the tenon tol take the barrel nuts, and it is easier to drill them at this stage through the solid, full-width neck, rather than do it later once the tenon in finished. The centres of the 10mm holes should be 6mm behind the line marking the neck/body joint. Use a brad-point drill in the drill press.

The timber either side of the tenon can be removed with a handsaw and cleaned up with a chisel but remember the cuts sideways into the neck need to follow the neck end angle and be at 90° to the centre of the neck. You want the non-tenon section of the heel to be in good contact with the front of the headblock.

The alternative is to use a bandsaw and router table. Remove most of the wood either side of the tenon to within 1mm or so of the tenon outline and the line marking the neck/body join and extending sideways a couple of millimetres past the neck width. This can be done easily, if carefully, on the bandsaw holding the bottom of the heel (the part at 90° to the end of the neck) on the bandsaw table. There should still beseveral millimetres of wood on either side of the two areas removed. Don't cut them off, as these are necessary for finishing off the tenon on the router table.

The waste section on either side of the tenon roughed out on the bandsaw

Cleaning up the tenon on the router table

The finished tenon and neckblock

Set up the router table with a long (I use a 1/4" spiral cut) bit that can extend exactly 20mm above the table. Run the flat end of the neck along the table, with the side of the heel block that is at 90° to the fingerboard surface along the table fence. Move the fence a millimetre or two at a time to gradually work in towards the tenon from the outside, remembering to feed the neck against the router rotation and keeping your fingers away from the bit as it emerges.

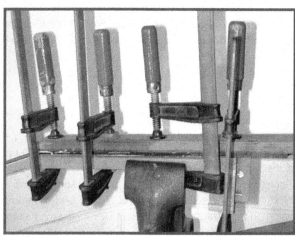

Gluing the fingerboard

Once the tenon is trimmed down to size, the wings outside the width of the fingerboard can be trimmed away along the side of the heel itself.

Fit the barrel nuts, which should be a firm push fit and align them so the threaded holes point at the 7mm holes. It can be useful to have a couple 75mm(3") bolts on hand to adjust the angle of the barrel nuts if necessary. These can be fed in through the body, threaded onto the barrel nuts and wiggled around to get the angle right with the tenon sitting outside the body. The 2" (50mm) bolts can now be fitted and the neck pulled into place with the bolts gently tightened.

Gluing the heelcap

Extend the lines marking the outside of the fretboard onto the body to the bridge position. If everything has worked right these lines should be equidistant from the centreline and the centreline of the neck should line up with the body centreline. If not, the flat ends of the neck on one side or other of the tenon will have to be carefully trimmed back with a chisel until the neck is in line. Be careful to keep the chisel cuts straight so the end of the neck sits flush with the end of the body. A slight undercut towards the tenon may be useful.

The neck carving fixture

Once the neck alignment is correct the back may be glued on and the fingerboard glued to the neck in the same way as described in the heel-less neck section. The bottom of the heel that was cut at 90° to the end of the neck before will need to be trimmed down to 3-4mm shorter than the body thickness and the angle adjusted to follow the tapering of the body. A cap of the same timber as the head overlay should be glued on. 3mm is a good thickness for this, with the option of also gluing on a contrasting veneer if that was done on the head.

The neck should be cut down to almost the width of the fingerboard on the bandsaw and trimmed to exact width either with chisels or on the router table as described previously. This won't obviously trim the full height of the heel which will need to be finished by hand. Fingerboard shaping and fretting should be done in the same way as for a heel-less neck, but it is useful to clamp a block with a slot cut for the tenon to the workbench to support the overhanging end of the fingerboard to keep it straight and give a solid base to hammer the frets in.

The shaft of the neck should be shaped by the faceting method also described previously, but here it is complicated by the heel. Having a rectangular end to the body, with the neck flush against it means the usual tapered heel looks quite strange and if kept at the full width of the headblock has to be very chunky. This design keeps the sides of the heel parallel to the fingerboard for 15mm and is then rounded off in a similar way to that used by Guild guitars. The front of the heel at the bottom extends another 10mm from the flat edges and can be curved or shaped any way you want. It gradually gets a bit thicker -another 3mm or so - closer to the neck shaft and then is flared into the neck profile.

The neck cross-section should be kept as far into the heel as possible to avoid a lumpy transition into the heel shape. It makes a little difference to the feel of the neck, but looks much more elegant.

The fitting of the fingerboard extension support for the archtop, if no lamination has been added to the soundboard, should be left until the body is bound and the final carving of the top is completed.

The fingerboard extender should be made from the same timber as the neck. It will be tapered from 5mm at the body join to around 10mm above the rosette. Sand the surface which will be glued to the bottom of the fingerboard flat and then fit the other side to the soundboard, which should have been carved and sanded to be as flat as possible. The end, which will be glued to the neck, needs to be cut or sanded to the correct angle.

If the fingerboard has been extended over the soundhole to get a couple of extra frets, the extender should be shaped to curve up from the rosette to the end of the fingerboard.

The main facets carved

*The neck carved
and sanded*

The basic frame of the instrument is formed by the sides glued to the neck and tail-blocks, re-enforced with the linings to which the soundboard and back are glued. The pivotal part of this structure is the neck block, where the sides top and back come together and to which the neck is also attached. This is the point of greatest stress, where the tension of the strings is trying to rotate the neck and neck block up and back towards the bridge.

The side assembly workboard

Over the years I have experimented with any number of different ways of holding the blocks and sides while gluing them together. I like the way a solid outside mould allows the builder to hold the sides firmly in position, and provides a solid surface to glue the blocks to the sides, especially with a guitar-bodied instrument. It is the critical nature of the side/neckblock joint of a teardrop-shaped instrument which has led to the development of this jig for assembling the body. Its origins are in the adjustable Spanish-style workboard, where the body outline is established by thick dowels attached by wingnuts on threaded inserts in radial slots on the workboard. A moveable curved clamping block allows the tailblock to be glued and clamped. Another clamping block at the neck end locates the neck block square to the centreline. Two vertical slots are cut, 4mm wide and 6mm deep, to allow the sides to overlap the block by a few millimetres when they are glued to the neck block. The width of this block holds two smaller shaped cauls which hold the sides to the neck block when gluing.

The front clamping block for a heel-less neck has a slanted face where the front of the body neck block is held. Using a heel-less neck, a square end to the body looks rather clunky, so the slanted end face of the body gives some suggestion of a heeled neck and flows the line of the neck into the shape of the body.

If using a neck with a heel, the end of this clamping block should be square to the workboard with an added 20mm wide block to locate the mortice in the neck block of the body.

This workboard can be used with either four-or five-course necks. If only one style of instrument was going to be built, solid sides to the mould could be made, but the separate shaped gluing cauls for the neckblock are recommended.

If the two clamping blocks are removed, the dowels can be used to hold the sides in shape after bending, until they are fully dried.

This kind of mould means building the body with the soundboard side down, so the top edge of the sides should always sit flat on the workboard. If they don't, the side has been twisted somewhere and another touch-up on the pipe may be needed, or an extra clamp to hold it in place.

The side assembly workboard

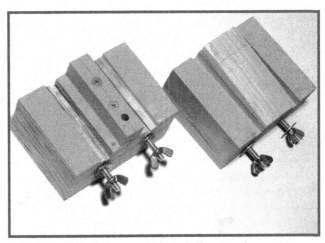

The two clamping blocks for different neck types

This book is describing two different ways of building the neck, so there are also two different ways of making a neck block. For the heel-less neck type there is a hollow neckblock, where the neck is bolted on from inside the body. For the tenon/barrel-nut type attachment with a neck heel, the neck block is solid and the same length as the bolts which fix the neck.

The hollow neck block

Mahogany or a similar timber is good this as it is both strong and reasonably light in weight. A piece of quartersawn mahogany 80mm long, 120mm wide and 40mm deep is needed. When the body outline was designed there should have been a 4mm allowance on either side of the neck where it joins the body

This allows the binding around the soundboard to continue to the end of the body, and be supported alongside the neck rebate. The outline of the neckblock will be 2mm inside the body outline, to allow for the thickness of the sides, and will be the same length as the extension of the neck into the body. The narrowest point of the neck block will be 4mm wider than the neck where it joins the body.

Making the hollow neck block

Square off one end of the block on a disk sander. This will be your reference edge for marking the centreline and final shape. Slice the mahogany block into two pieces, so you have one a little over 25mm thick leaving the other around 13mm thick. Plane the thick piece to 25mm, mark on it a centreline and trace the outline of the block. Mark the neck width from the front of the block to the back of the neck which will be 70mm. Using my standard four-course neck dimensions, the neck width will increase from around 46mm to 48mm over this distance, but check your neck for the exact width from the body join to the end of the block.

If making a flat-top instrument the mortice can be cut at this stage. Draw lines parallel to the neck edges out near the edge of the block and sand or plane the edges of the block to the line. This allows you now to cut the neck mortice using saw and chisel or on a router table. If the neck (excluding the fingerboard) is 18mm thick, and the soundboard is 2.5mm thick, rout out a 15.5mm deep mortice.

Hog out most of the wood with a large (18mm or so) forstner bit in the drill press keeping a couple of millimetres away from the edges and keeping the centre point of the bit shallower than the required depth. With a straight router bit, gradually remove the excess. Start in the middle of the mortice and move the fence only 3-4mm at a time until the tapered mortice is the correct width.

An archtop mortice is rather more complex, as it will get shallower towards the end of the neck. The soundboard beess to have been constructed so the overall height can be measured and the neck angle calculated. Laying it out on paper is the best way to go about it and the diagram on the next page shows a typical setup.

A line extended along the top of the neck (without the fingerboard) should finish 10mm above the soundboard at the saddle position or around 17mm continuing a line along the top of the frets down the centre of the fingerboard. Allow 3-5mm from the bottom of the fingerboard to the top of the soundboard at the neck join. The neck, without the fingerboard is 18mm thick, so the front depth of the mortice will be 13-15mm, depending on how much of the neck over-stands above the general level of the soundboard.

The first stage in constructing the hollow neckblock

The completed hollow neckblock

The angle of the mortice can be calculated from the drawing, but there can be some error. Take the depth at the end of the neck (closest to the soundhole) and rout out the mortice to that depth only, using the method described above. Cut the rest of the mortice down to a little under the calculated depth at the neck end with a fine saw and chisels. Final adjustments to the depth can be made when fitting the neck.

From a small piece of 12mm (1/2") plywood make a block which is the same size as the neck section which fits into the body. For the archtop neck shape it to fit the angle of the mortice. Clamp it to the workboard exactly centred on the head clamping block and drill holes for two locating pins (I use short offcuts of the 3/16" steel rod used for the trussrod, but almost anything will do)

Alternative 1 - make this top section in three pieces, a bottom 10mm thick with two cheeks glued on that follow the neck outline. A tapered bottom section should work for the archtop block once you establish the size graphically. The 12mm (1/2") piece of plywood cut to the shape of that section of the neck and clamped to the bottom section will align the cheeks. This plywood block will also be used when gluing the sides to the finished block.

Alternative 2 - You can leave this top section of the block solid and rout the mortice fully out later, but this can be an exciting procedure, needs a a big router and disaster is never very far away.

Trim the block to the outline drawn on before, allowing 1-2mm outside the lines for final shaping after the block is glued together.

Angling the front of the block back around 7° gives some visual suggestion of a traditional neck heel. This makes getting all the angles right rather more complex and the front clamping block on the workboard has had a tapered wedge glued on to securely hold the head block when gluing the sides on.

Plane the thinner piece to 10mm thick and cut that out to the profile of the block in the same way as the top section.

Now comes the tricky bit. I think it looks better, and saves a little weight, to have the bottom section of the neckblock (the part that the back is glued to) following the line of the back. The back is essentially a section of a 15 foot radius sphere, which is glued to the sides of the instrument which reduce in height from 80mm at the tailblock to 70mm at the neckblock, so the mathematics of describing the changing heights of the sides is scary to even contemplate, but we don't have to. We can get away with just considering a 15 foot radius curve along the centreline of the back

There is a 35mm gap at the front of the block between the top and bottom sections which expands by around 4mm at the end of the block. Another small piece of mahogany 10mm thick and as long as the width of the neckblock (plus a couple of mm for final shaping) and a little over 35mm wide is needed as the front support. Sand a 7° angle on one edge and a 10° angle on the other. The side view of the block in the plans section should make it obvious Make two 13mm x 13mm mahogany strips around 50mm long, and sand one end square. These are the rear supports.

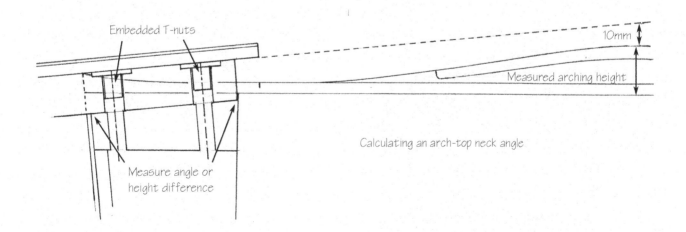

Embedded T-nuts

10mm

Measured arching height

Measure angle or height difference

Calculating an arch-top neck angle

Glue the 7° side of the front support to the upper section of the block. A rubbed glue joint will work fine here. When that is dried, lightly clamp the bottom section, without any glue, and trim the rear supports to a gentle push fit. Position the rear supports so they overlap the outline a few mm and mark their position with a pencil. Run a thin bead of glue along the 10° edge of the front support, a drop on each end of the rear supports, and clamp the lot together. Don't let the bits slide around too much.

When the glue has set find a piece of side offcut or similar to glue onto the front of the block. This is just a decorative cover for the block, and is a good way to use up those highly figured little bits of wood which are just too nice to throw out.

Once it is all dry the block can be trimmed down to the pencilled outline, working off the top surface of the top block as the index. Use a disk sander to sand the front and back surfaces, and a drum sander to shape the sides. It can be done with a plane and sanding blocks, but the power tools are quicker and more accurate.

Solid neck block

This type of block is similar to the traditional guitar neck block, except that the block is to the body outline so that once the sides are glued to it, its narrowest width is the same as the neck width where the neck joins the body. A piece, solid or laminated, of mahogany 50mm long, 110mm wide and 80mm deep is needed. Decide on the top surface and square off the front and back, the end grain, to 50mm. This a standard length for the bolts that attach the neck with the barrel nuts in the neck tenon, and also gives sufficient gluing surface for the sides, top and back. The block can be extended on each side to allow more gluing surface for the sides, so the inside has a concave shape.

Using the top surface as the index, mark centrelines on all four surfaces, and trace the outline of the shape onto the bottom surface. The 20x20mm mortice for the neck tenon is cut at this point and a matching block attached to the centre of the inside of the front clamping block on the workboard to locate the block when gluing on the sides. The mortice can be roughly cut a little small on the bandsaw and brought up to size on the router table. Bandsaw out the shape of the block and sand to the required outline.

The sides

A pair of sides bought from a lutherie supplier will be two bookmatched pieces of wood usually around 4-5mm thick, and long and wide enough for a guitar. These have to be reduced in thickness to 2mm (.080"). Suppliers will often offer a thicknessing service, and for a small cost this can save a good deal of effort and time.

Traditionally the sides have been thicknessed with planes and scrapers. This needs a well-sharpened and set-up plane as well as a sharp scraper. Sides for a bouzouki don't need to be as large as needed for a guitar, so if thicknessing them by hand it is easier to trim them down to 700mm long by 85mm wide before starting the planing process. Before doing this look at the grain patterns and direction and establish where the tail joint will be, as well as the edge which will meet the top. If the timber has noticeable changes in colour or pattern, try to bookmatch them as closely as possible at the tail joint. Plane a straight line along the edge of the sides that will meet the soundboard. This can be done on a shooting board, or with a shooting plane held upside down in a vice.

Chances are the grain will not run perfectly straight along the length of the wood - there will be runout - and it will be necessary to determine in which direction the wood can be safely planed. Clamp a side along the edge of the workbench on the end closest to you and start planing as close to the clamp as possible. Once you have the surface of the wood smooth except for the area around the clamp, move the clamp to the far end and smooth the area where the clamp was originally. Flip the wood over and repeat the process on the other side.

A solid neckblock on the assembly workboard

Once both sides of the wood have been planed, check to see if the previous decision about bookmatching were correct. Scrap and sand the outsides to be as smooth as possible as any chips or weak points can be the start of a crack when bending. Once the outsides are smooth and defect-free, do the rest of the thicknessing on the inside surface.

When getting close to final thickness be careful planing towards the clamp, as 2mm thick wood can be quite fragile. Remove the plane marks with the scraper and 80 grit sandpaper.

By the time you have most woods down to 2mm thick they are becoming quite flexible, almost like cardboard. The wood gets to the point where it is suddenly much floppier than it was when it was a fraction thicker. That is the point to stop.

Alternatively, find another luthier or woodworker who has a thickness sander (sometimes called an abrasive planer). Just about every professional or semi-professional guitar builder will have one. There are a number of cantilever 16″ drum sanders available, either original American designs or Taiwanese clones, which will do any number of useful jobs in a luthier's workshop.

Cutting the sides to shape

The plans include a template for the sides, with one straight edge and one curved edge. The soundboard is glued to the straight edge and the curved edge allows for the tapering depth of the body and the longitudinal and lateral curvature of the back.

Lay the two thicknessed sides on the bench, outside surface up, with the edges that will be the top of the instrument alongside each other. You should be able to see bookmatched grain patterns and if you can't flip one of the sides around until the grain is best matched. Mark the edges that will be glued to the soundboard.

Trace the side templates onto the sides and cut out to within 1-2mm of the curved line. DO NOT cut them to the correct length at this time as this will make it very hard to accurately bend the sides towards the ends. Leave 50mm (2″) at each end.

Side bending

Teardrop bouzouki sides are rather easier to bend than a guitar, not having a pronounced waist and the complex changing from concave to convex curves. The traditional way to bend sides is around a hot pipe, which can be as simple as a 300mm (1 foot) length of 60-70mm (2.5″) copper or brass pipe held in a vice and heated with a propane torch. The pipe has a brass bracket pop-riveted to one end, with most of the other end closed off with another piece of brass sheet riveted to it. The bracket can be held in a vice, with a couple of pieces of scrap wood as insulation and the propane torch mounted at the right height with a simple plywood support. The pipe can be used horizontally or vertically.

The first question any stringed instrument maker gets asked is how the sides are bent, and it is a delightfully simple and satisfying process - though most builders now use some form of heated mould such as the two described on the next page.

Laying out the side template on a side

A modified version of the Fox side bender is simple to build and works very effectively, powered by 2 x 150watt and 1 x 100 watt light bulbs.

A third approach is a silicon heating blanket over a simple mould. These are thin rubber sheets embedded with heating elements which can be bought in any desired size. They heat up within a minute or so and can cook a side into shape within 10-15 minutes.

Hot pipe bending

Even if using one of the heated mould techniques, a hot pipe will still usually be necessary to refine the final shape of the side curves, so it is an essential technique to learn.

Start by marking the outside of each side using a pencil or white grease (Chinagraph) pencil that won't disappear when the wood is dampened. Use an arrow at one end or the other and a couple of arrows pointing to the soundboard edge so as not to get the orientation of the sides mixed up.

Mount the pipe in a vice, with the propane torch in the open end. The pipe has to be hot enough so that when water is dropped on it it bounces off in little droplets. If the water just stays and sizzles it is not hot enough. Wet the sides - a laundry trigger pump sprayer works well - and start the bending with the concave section around the neckblock. Allowing a 50mm overlap at the each end means the centre of the neckblock curve will be about 100mm from the neck end of the side.

Rock the wood over the plate with a gentle bending pressure and it will bend. As the wood dries, spray on more water until the correct curve is bent. Have a half body template as well as the neckblock on the bench nearby to check the curves. Work with the top edge of the side following the template.

Once the neckblock curve is right, flip the side over and start bending the long curve of the body from the inside. The trickiest part of this is where the concave curve becomes convex, and care must be taken to make this transition as smooth as possible.

Take care to keep the sides bent in the same plane, so that when the side is sitting on the top edge it is vertical to the bench. It is easy to twist the side when bending and this will make it difficult to then glue in the blocks.

Once fully bent, clamp the sides in the gluing jig and let dry at least overnight. There is usually some springback, so a touch-up the next day is likely to be needed.

Side benders

If a light bulb powered Fox-style bender is used start by wetting the side and holding it to the high point of the mould under the stainless steel strip with the spring caul, making sure it is running parallel to the sides of the mould and attach the block to form the concave front curve. Turn the light bulbs on and allow it to heat up for a few minutes. Slowly, over a few minutes, wind down the block until the side is clamped right down in the concave section of the mould. Pull the spring-loaded caul down to the other end and leave for 20-30 minutes until the water has been steamed off, the wood starts smelling 'cooked'. Turn the lights off and leave overnight. Adjust the curve to the template the next day with the hot pipe.

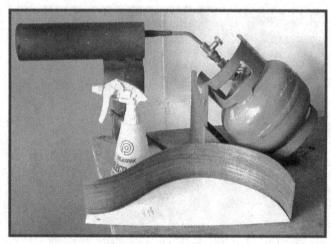
Bending sides on a hot pipe

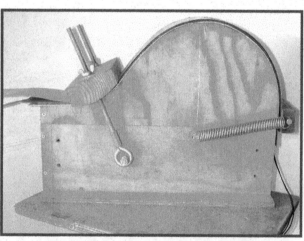
The sides bender in operation, suitable for heating with either light bulbs or a silicon rubber heat blanket

A similar mould and technique can be used with a heat blanket, though a solid mould made from MDF is just as effective with cutouts made to allow several cauls to hold using clamps or rubber bands the side and blanket in place while it cooks. Start at the neckblock curve and wrap the rest of the side around the mould. This will only need around 10 minutes of cooking.

The tailblock

The tail block can be made of a solid piece of 12mm mahogany (or similar) or 12mm plywood. The disadvantage in a solid tailblock made with the grain following the sides is that there is some danger of splitting from an impact and if made with the grain at right angles to the sides, the top and back must be glued to endgrain, which is not as effective a glue joint. A good quality pine ply works well, but an alternative is laminating three pieces of spruce to make a lightweight but strong block. The two outside pieces are 5mm thick with the grain following that of the sides with a 3mm piece in the middle with the grain at right angles.

They are glued up oversize and trimmed to 50mm wide and a couple of mm higher than the height of the sides. Draw and centreline on one side and shape the other on the disk-sander to match the curve of the sides. The centreline on the inside is useful when both gluing the side and for lining up the soundboard when that is glued in place.

Gluing the neckblock and tailblock

Before gluing the sides to the neck and tail blocks they have to be trimmed to length. With the top clamping block removed, lightly clamp the sides to the dowel outline, and mark the centreline at the tail and the front edge of the neckblock. Get the sides fitting as snugly to the dowels as possible all the way around, as this will ensure a neat joint at the tailblock. A miscalculation of a couple of mm here doesn't really matter, but any more might mean an over-large centre insert where the sides join at the tail. Mark a 90° line from the top edge at the tail end of the sides at the pencil marks and trim. Replace the top clamping block.

The slots in the top clamping block allow a 6mm or so overlap, so trim them a little longer so they butt up to the end of the slots in the head clamping block. Check for fit again, making sure the sides are touching all the dowels. If you get it exactly right the slight spring pressure of the butting together at the tail and the head-clamping block will push the sides firmly against the dowels.

Remove the sides and fit the neckblock over the tapered ply block (if using a heel-less neck) or the 20mm extension (for a heeled neck) to hold it centred on the workboard. If you are using Rosewood sides, wipe them down with acetone where both blocks will be glued. Apply glue to the sides of the head block. Fit the sides into position again. Fix a large clamp lengthways to hold the block against the clamping block, making sure it is also sitting flat on the workboard. Fit the curved clamping cauls and clamp.

Smear glue on the curved side of the tailblock, line the pencilled centreline up with the workboard centreline and clamp in place. Leave overnight to dry.

Trimming the sides to length

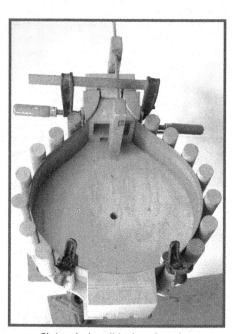
Gluing the headblock to the sides

The linings

As with most other stringed instruments there is a need for linings to give more gluing surface when gluing the top and back in position. There are a number of ways this can be done.

In the traditional Spanish method of guitar construction, the soundboard is placed face down on the workboard, the sides are held in place and small triangular pieces of wood (tentalones) glued on to hold the two together. This was a rubbed joint and either animal glue or Titebond can be used. This still a good way to do it, especially for a flat-top instrument (harder for an archtop), provided that the slight arch of the soundboard is supported around the edges and the soundboard is clamped in place using a block bolted through the soundhole.

An alternative, and my preference, is gluing on both top and bottom linings and shaping the contour of the back with a dished sanding form before gluing the soundboard.

Linings can be solid or kerfed. If solid they should be laminated out of three layers of 2mm thick timber 12-15mm high for the top to give a finished thickness of 6mm. Classical guitars often just use one 3mm-thick solid lining for the back. They should be pre-bent to shape and clamped in place with clothes pegs or other spring clamps.

Kerfed linings are made from mahogany or similar timber and cut to 7x15mm (though 6x12mm would be fine). Triangular cross-section linings can be bought from instrument-making suppliers, and there are some available with a veneer on the back which stops splitting around tight curves. They are not hard to make in the workshop with a simple bandsaw jig to cut the kerfs. The length of each strip is limited by the size of the bandsaw.

A variation on kerfed linings is to make the kerfed strips for the top edge more rectangular and glue them with the kerfed side to the sides, leaving the uncut web side facing inside the instrument. Lutherie teacher Charles Fox suggests this makes a more rigid frame.

With the sides cut close to their finished shape for the back curve before bending, the back linings can be glued first with the side and block assembly still on the workboard. A little over half a metre (20" or so) of linings are needed for each side, top and back. Trim one end so it sits flush against the back of the neckblock, smear with glue and clamp to the sides with cloth pegs re-enforced with rubber bands. If short strips are used, butt the ends together and try for a tight fit against the sides of the tailblock.

Leave overnight to dry and flip the side assembly over and repeat for the top edge, overlapping the side by a mm or so. When that is dry, plane and sand down flush, being careful to keep the top edge of the side in the one plane without any dips in the middle. Flip the side assembly over again so the top edge sits on the workboard (which is a good way to check if the top edge is flat) and shape the back curve.

Gluing the tailblock

A section of kerfed lining being glued with rubber-band re-enforced clothespegs

The dowels can be removed from the jig at this point, as the linings should hold the sides assembly in shape at this stage. A few 25-37mm (1"-1.5") dowels can be used to keep the assembly from sliding around while sanding the curve of the back

The sides are shaped to fit the back which is a segment of a 15 foot radius sphere. The back braces are shaped to that curve which gives the transverse shape, but the back must be pushed into the curve longitudinally when glued on. A 15 foot radius dished workboard is simple to make and described in the section on jigs.

The dished workboard is covered with 60grit strips of sandpaper, glued on with contact cement or a latex glue. It is rotated on a vertical axis which can be a length of steel tube (a piece of curtain rod) or thick dowel with holes to match drilled on the centre of the form and the centre of the workboard.

Rotate the form, checking progress regularly and measure the side height at opposite points to keep the sides even. The neck block should have been projecting a few mm above the sides when the sides were glued, and the shaping process can be speeded up with a block plane or chisels removing the sanded areas bit by bit.

By the time the 80mm tail depth and 70mm neck end depth is reached, both blocks and the full length of all the linings on both sides should show sanding marks all over.

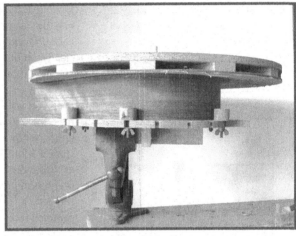

Sanding the back curve

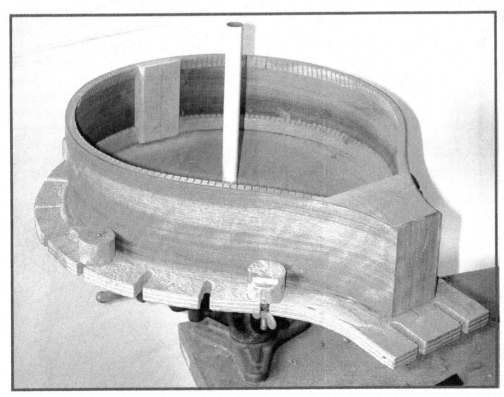

The completed side assembly

The flat-top soundboard is made in a similar way to a steel string guitar from 2 bookmatched pieces of spruce or other suitable wood, 2-3mm thick with braces glued on the inside which both stiffen the soundboard and distribute the pull of the glued-on bridge. The strings are held by tapered pins through the bridge which lock the ball-ends of the strings to a hardwood plate.

Joining and thicknessing the soundboard

The soundboard material will come from the supplier as two pieces of spruce (or whatever you are using), sequentially cut from the same billet of wood and around 5mm thick. It should be relatively simple to determine the order in which they were cut by saw marks and/or grain patterns by holding the two pieces together and looking at the sides and the end grain. It may be necessary to take a thin slice off each end and sand it to see the end grain clearly. (Rough saw marks and a sealing compound can obscure the end grain.)

A perfect pair of soundboard halves will have the annual rings vertical across the entire width of the boards and evenly spaced 1.5 to 2.5mm apart. What is sold as lower-quality board may have the ring spacing more variable or drifting off the vertical towards one side. Once the common face of the boards is established they can be opened up like the pages of a book and the grain pattern will be a mirror image either side of what will be the centre join.

Trim the edges to be joined so the grain is running as close as possible to the line of the join. This can be done with a plane or it may be easier to slice a wedge off on the bandsaw. Mark with a couple of pencil lines across what will end up being the face of soundboard and the centre joint. The length can be trimmed to 50mm (2") longer than the finished bouzouki soundboard (which will usually be smaller than the guitar-sized pieces that come from the suppliers) and the outside edges trimmed allowing 15-20mm wider on each side than the finished soundboard. This not necessary unless you are worried about the amount of hand thicknessing to be done, and the extra length is useful for the back centre strip.

With a lower-quality pair of soundboard halves, choose as the centre joint the edges with the closest annual ring spacing and/or the most vertical annual rings. Variation in the annual ring spacing is more aethestic rather than relating to the quality of sound produced, but it is important that the end grain be as vertical as possible in the centre of the soundboard as when the rings are off the vertical this means that the wood has less cross-grain stiffness - is floppier across the width of the board. This will make the centre of the soundboard stiffer than the outside, which is preferable.

Planing the edge of a soundboard before gluing.

To join the two halves of the soundboard it is essential that a perfectly straight edge be planed (or perhaps sanded). A shooting board and a long jointing plane is the best way. The cutting edge of the plane blade should should be straight and parallel to the sole of the plane. Set a reasonably coarse cut and get a clean edge on the soundboard halves. Try to plane a very slightly concave curve. This needs only be .5mm or so, but means the next step will be slowly taking this out until the edge is perfectly straight. Set the plane to a much finer cut and take successive cuts until an even ribbon is sliced off. The trick is to keep the plane's sole in firm contact with the wood and not let it rock at the beginning and end of the cut.

Hold the two halves up to the light, and check the join. A small sliver of light in the middle is acceptable (if not really desirable), but any gap at the ends means a return to the shooting board.

If a jointing plane is not available the joint can be done with a smoothing plane and a sanding jig on the shooting board. The sanding jig can be made simply from a straight length of metal angle screwed to a piece of ply or MDF and faced with 120 grit sandpaper glued on with rubber cement.
Alternatively the side of a spirit level can

be used similarly. Get the edges of the soundboard halves as straight as possible with the plane and then finish off with the sanding jig. Check the join in the same way as mentioned previously. When the two edges can be held up with no light showing between them, give the sanded edges a going over with a stiff brush to remove the dust and then perhaps a wipe down with a rag dampened with alcohol. This is a critical joint on the instrument and it must be as clean and tight as possible.

There are lots of ways to join soundboards (and backs) with some wonderfully complicated jigs. The venerable Spanish method of ropes and wedges works as well as any and is simpler than most. It consists of six dressed 2"x1" (50mm x 25mm) pieces of wood around 600mm (2') long, three tapered wedges around the same length and a few metres of non-stretching rope. Rub a candle over the centre of each piece of wood to stop any glue squeezeout sticking. Place three of the 2x1 sticks on the shooting board (so the middle is supported and the ends are free) so that the soundboard halves will extend 50mm (2") past the outside sticks.

Place the soundboard halves with the marked, outside face downwards on the

sticks and put the other three sticks on top. Make a loop in one end of the rope, attach it around one end pair of sticks and wrap it twice around each pair of sticks in a figure-of-eight pattern, crossing over in the middle of the top stick.

Keep the rope as taut as possible and tie it off around the other end pair of sticks. Insert the wedges under the rope and tap in until everything tightens up. Practice this first without any glue and then disassemble and repeat with a bead of glue along one edge. Rub the glued edges together to get an even spread of glue and then wrap and wedge. Before the final tapping in of the wedges adjust the alignment along the join by pushing with the fingers so that the two pieces overlap as little as possible. Leave the ends a couple of millimetres out of alignment so there is a visual reference to the centre join. Once the soundboard is thicknessed the centre join can sometimes be quite hard to see, and the notches at each end allow the centreline to be quickly established.

Let the glue dry overnight, as the moisture in the glue will swell the joint slightly, and thicknessing before this moisture has escaped will mean a dip appearing along the joint the next day.

The soundboard must now be reduced down to around 2.5mm. A little thicker -3mm- for Western Red Cedar or Redwood or a very soft, light spruce. By far the easiest way is with a thickness sander, but it is satisfying to do it by hand with a plane. A sharp, well set up smoothing plane with a very slightly convex edge to the blade is best. The soundboard should be clamped firmly to the workbench with the outside face upward after cleaning up any glue squeezeout with a chisel or scraper. The almost inevitable slight runout of the grain will mean that each half of the soundboard can only be safely planed in one direction.

Set the plane for a fairly fine cut and start smoothing out the saw marks on one side

Gluing the soundboard halves

of the soundboard, being careful around the centre join. Once the first half of the soundboard is smooth, rotate the board 180° and repeat for the other half. With the half-sheet sanding board, faced with 120 grit paper, finish levelling and smoothing of the outside face of the soundboard.

Turn the soundboard over and repeat for the inside face. Be sure to clean off the bench before placing the finished outside face of the soundboard on it. It is important to be as careful as possible with the outside face of the soundboard from this point on. It takes only a small piece of grit or a chip of wood to imprint a hard-to-remove ding or dent in the softwood.

Once the inside face is smoothed with the plane, check the thickness with the dial gauge caliper. Note the thickness with a pencil over the whole area every 20-30mm and repeat the planing and measuring until just a little thicker than your required final thickness. Finish off with the half-sheet sanding board.

Draw the centre line on both sides and trace the outline on the outside face. Cut it out on the bandsaw, allowing 3mm outside the outline.

The Soundhole and Rosette

The rosette around the soundhole is both decorative and adds structural strength in

that area of the soundboard. There is no need for the soundhole to be circular, but it is the easiest shape to cut. An important factor is the ability to get a hand inside the instrument for doing things like installing pickups and to facilitate any repairs sometime in the future.

Graham Caldersmith tells me that the air in the soundhole is coupled reflexively to the fundamental mode of top vibration. Sometimes the fundamental back vibration will also couple with the air in the soundhole lowering the air resonance further. While this might be a good thing sometimes, in general Caldersmith suggests that stiffer back bracing is preferable.

Changing the area of the soundhole will affect the air resonance of the box. Decreasing the area of the soundhole will lower the air resonance and increasing it will raise it.

In the absence of very much experimental work on soundhole sizes and their effect on the sound, the 80mm soundhole size for these instruments is really what looks

right for the body size when compared to that of a guitar and it seems to work.

As a visit to a guitar shop will show, there are any number of ways that the soundhole rosette can be made. Classical guitars use a complex construction of mosaic tiles and veneer rings, while most steel-string guitars use one or more concentric rings of various purflings. My preferred style is a solid 10mm wide ring of either the same material as the body or the bindings, with the inside of the ring the edge of the soundhole and purflings on the outside that match those around the soundboard. Feel free to be as inventive as you wish.

NOTE: from this point all gluing procedures on the soundboard should be done with a relative humidity of 40-45%. Failure to do this will result in the convex soundboard becoming concave in periods of low humidity.

The neck edge of the soundhole should be 80mm from the end of the body. This allows 70mm for the heel-less neck mortice with another 10mm clear away

Cutting out the solid rosette ring

from the soundhole edge. This also allows 22 frets clear of the soundhole while allowing the possibility of another 2 frets on a fingerboard extension. Mark the centre of the soundhole another 40mm away and drill a hole to suit whatever circle cutter is available. A matching hole is cut in the rectangular workboard which will allow the circle cutter to rotate and be held securely.

A 110-120mm square piece of 2mm thick timber for the rosette should be glued to a slightly larger piece of ply or MDF with a drop of glue in the centre.

When dry, drill a hole for the circle cutter and mount the circle cutter in the drill press on a slow (350 rpm) rotational speed. Cut out a circle with a 40mm inside

radius and a 50mm outside radius. Cut the outside first and then reverse the cutter blade to cut the ring free.

Check the finished diameter of the rosette ring, and mark the inside diameter on the soundboard as well as the outside diameter plus whatever purflings you want to use. Fit the circle cutter through the hole in the soundboard and the matching hole in the workboard and clamp the soundboard in place. Cut a circle on the inside mark around 1.5mm deep.

Check that the ring just sits outside the inner cut and repeat for the outside circle cut. A cleaner cut will be made by rotating the cutter away from the centre

line, rather than trying to just rotate it in a circle. A few more cuts between the two outside cuts will make chiselling out the waste to a constant depth of 1.5mm rather easier. Keep in mind the grain runout and be careful not let the chisel slip and cut into the outside of the channel.

This a job which can be easily done with a router or a Dremel and there are several jigs available for the Dremel.

Check the fit of the wood ring and the purflings. They want to be a press fit in to the channel. If the channel is too small, use the cutter to slightly enlarge it. If it is too

Installing the rosette

big you will have to rethink the purfling and possibly add a strip to fill the channel. Unclamp the soundboard from the workboard. Glue the rosette in place, with minimal glue to minimise squeezeout, using a piece of perspex as a clamping caul and a matching piece of ply or MDF underneath the soundboard, using as many cam clamps as can fit.

Leave to dry overnight and remove the excess of the rosette down to the level of the soundboard with a block plane and chisels, being careful not to cut into

the surrounding spruce. Finish off with the sanding board. With the soundboard clamped to the workboard again cut out the soundhole with the circle cutter. Cut most of the way through from the outside and then turn the soundboard over and complete the cut from the inside.

With 120 grit sandpaper slightly round over the inside of the soundhole and clean up any glue around the inside of the rosette.

Bracing the soundboard

As previously discussed there are any number of ways to brace the soundboard.

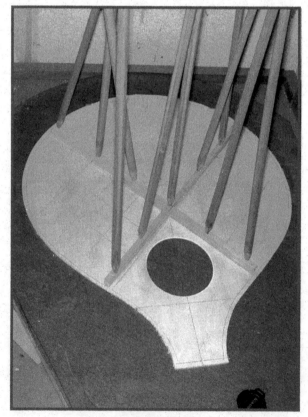
Gluing the X brace

This hybrid X/lattice brace system is just one possibility but it works.

The first step is to mark out the bracing pattern on the inside of the soundboard. Draw an outline of the bridge in its correct position, and draw in the 6x12mm X braces so the centre of each arm crosses over each rear corner of the bridge and the upper arms of the braces are at least 10mm from the edge of the soundhole. The crossover angle should be 90°.

On steel string guitars the angle of the X braces is a useful way of controlling the stiffness of the soundboard. Opening up the angle will loosen the soundboard, giving a stronger bass, while closing the angle down will stiffen the soundboard for a brighter sound. The lattice bracing around the X is stiffening up the entire centre of the soundboard in any case using this design while still allowing the X braces to spread the string load through the bridge.

The bridge plate is made from a hardwood such as rosewood, maple or Tasmanian blackwood and acts as both a stop for the string ball ends and as a stiffening element in the middle of the soundboard. The grain runs across the soundboard and the plate should extend 5mm in front and behind the bridge.

The lattice is made from 3x6mm spruce at 40mm centres, measured from the X brace intersection, and running parallel to the X braces. The lattice should end 35mm from the linings. There are also two 6x6mm braces which run from the neckblock to the X braces to strengthen the area around the soundhole.

All the braces are made from quartersawn spruce, with the grain vertical to the soundboard.

The X braces are the first to be made and glued. Two pieces of 6x12mm spruce 320mm long are needed. One edge needs to be arched to a 25' radius curve.

The plans include an arching template, and this be done done on a disc or belt sander. Alternatively, a jig can be made for a ball bearing guide router bit on the router table. A block plane or a chisel can be used, but care must be taken to keep the arched surface at right angles to the vertical sides of the braces. It is useful to write a number on one end of each and reperat that on the soundboard at the end of each brace.

The braces have to be notched at their intersection. Place the X braces on the positioning liner on the soundboard and mark the points where the braces intersect on both sides of each brace. Draw vertical lines from the non-arched surface and mark the bottoms of each notch halfway (which should be 6mm from the top surface). Remember the notch has to be cut on the arched surface of one brace and the opposite side of the other. Hold the braces in a vice and use a razor saw to cut down to the marked halfway points.

With the brace sitting flat on the workbench, use a 6mm chisel to remove the waste sections and check how they fit together. They want to be a gentle press fit, and the arched surfaces should meet at the intersection. Adjust the width and depth of the notches with the chisel if necessary.

Run a little glue into one of the notches and press together. Run a bead of glue along the arched surface of each brace and smear with a fingertip so the entire surface is covered. Position the braces on the soundboard and clamp. This can be done on the 25' dished workboard and go-sticks or with a number of cam clamps. Clean up any glue squeezeout, and leave for at least an hour to dry.

Shape the braces to a pointed arch cross-section and scallop the ends from the back of the bridge and from halfway from the intersection to the top end. They should taper away to nothing at the point

where they meet the linings. Sand with 120 grit paper.

Make a bridge plate from a piece of 3mm hardwood (an offcut from the back is useful) Make clamping caul from a piece of 12mm ply or MDF. This can be arched to match the brace curve, by rubbing it over the sheet of sandpaper held onto the dished workboard, but this is not essential. Glue with cam clamps or go-sticks and clean up any glue squeezeout.

Cut nine lengths of 3x6mm lattice for braces numbered 1-5 on the soundboard half plan at the back of the book. (Nine because there are four on the other half of the soundboard). They can be slightly

arched on the gluing surface by around .5mm, but they are flexible enough for it not to really matter. Run a thin covering of glue along the bottom of each brace as well as the end which meets the X brace and rub them into position. Where they cross the bridge plate notch them so they overlap 3mm.

Give the glue a couple of minutes to grab and then clamp with two strips of wood 4-6mm thick which are long enough to span across all three braces. Clamp or go-stick between the braces. They are so

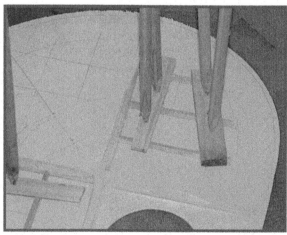

Gluing the lattice

narrow that it is hard to effectively clamp them individually.

When dry, taper all the braces away to nothing at a point 35mm from the linings.

Cut short pieces of the 3x6mm stock to fill in the lattice which are numbered 6-9 on the plan. These need to be a snug fit between the longer lattice arms, and can be clamped in the same way. When dry taper these in the same way, effectively forming a domed surface to the lattice.

Hold the soundboard in a bottom quarter and tap in the middle to hear the # 5 mode or ring mode resonance and where the tail block will be glued to hear the #2 mode, which should be around an octave lower. The #5 mode should be around E or 134Hz. A full tone on either side is not too much of a problem, but any higher means the stiffness of the soundboard should be reduced. This can be done by scalloping out the main X brace between the bridge and the intersection and/or removing a little more of the lattice both in width and height. Do this gradually and the pitch of the #5 mode should drop to within the hoped-for range.

The two 6x6mm soundhole braces are glued on after the side assembly is glued to the soundboard.

Soundboard Resonances

Measuring the main resonance of the soundboard is a process which is done at successive stages of the making the soundboard. The soundboard was held

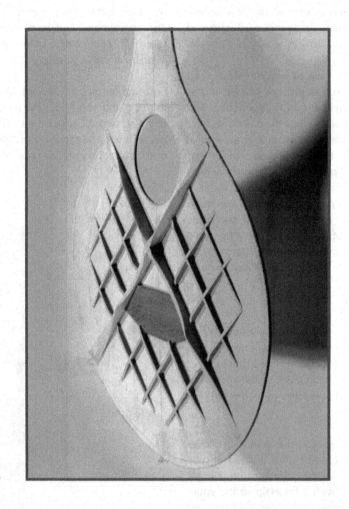

around the position marked with an X in the first picture and tapped in the middle. This excites the number 5 mode as a free plate. A Conn Strobotuner was used to determine the note produced and I don't really worry about what octave the note is, more the way it goes up and down as braces are added and carved away.

Thicknessed to 2.5mm and cut to shape the resonance was a G. This dropped to B when the rosette was installed and the soundhole cut. When 6x12mm X-braces were glued on it rose again to between F and F#. Profiling the braces and scolloping the ends did little to the frequency, except getting a resonance an octave higher (which puzzled me). Adding the 6 x 3mm lattice and a carving them down to a overall dome shape took the tap-tone up to G, and then scalloping the X braces between the crossover point and the bridge down to 6mm high brought the note down to the E.

Once the soundboard was glued to the side assembly the pitch rose once again to somewhere between B and C, dropping to slightly above B when the outside 40-50mm of the soundboard were thinned down to 2mm at the edges. The outside perimeter of the lattice was brought in around 5mm and evened up and another couple of mm were scalloped out of the X braces.

The note dropped to between B and A# and I stopped at that point. When the back was glued on the air resonance (obtained by humming into the soundhole) was around C#. When the lacquer was applied and the bridge glued it stayed much

the same, perhaps creeping up a small amount. Checking back to the notes made on instruments built over the past few years, these frequencies are in the generally expected range.

Through the generosity of the physics department of the Australian Defence Force Academy, I was able to excite the flat-top soundboard with a loudspeaker and a frequency generator. The soundboard showed strong resonances at

the frequencies in the pictures

The 138hz resonance is the E that I noted when tapping the finished soundboard. The strong shapes will be higher resonant modes. There were other resonances as well, but these where the most definite ones.

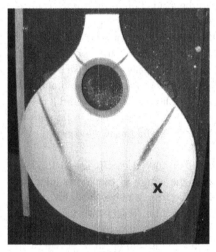

138Hz

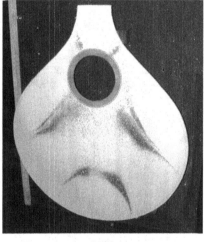

241Hz

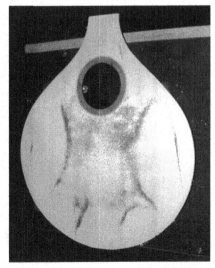

370Hz

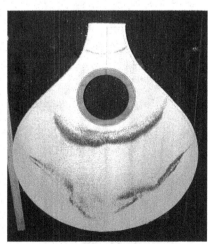

504Hz

The mould is a piece of 18mm plywood cut to 50mm larger than the body shape. The hump in the centre starts 25mm inside the body outline and is shaped in a smooth curve flattening out on the top. This can be made from either 18mm plywood or 18mm MDF. The bridge position is around the middle of hump.The finished inside arch height won't be quite 18mm high because of the springback of the timber, but around a 15mm is usual.

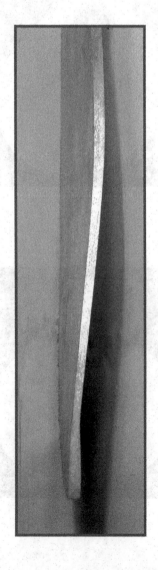

Draw a centreline down the middle of the mould as this assists in lining up the soundboard halves when clamping. At the top of the mould, 10-15mm outside the body shape and 25mm each side of the centre line drill two 6mm holes halfway through the ply and make up two pins from 6mm dowel with pointed ends that stand around 25mm proud of the mould surface. These pins will locate the soundboard halves when clamping.

The clamping caul is also made from 18mm ply, and faced with cork. It is 40mm wide, half outside and half inside the body outline and this gives a little room on the inside before the spruce is forced into the curve. I used offcuts from cork floor tiles about 6mm thick for the facing. This lessens the chance of crushing the spruce, especially at the initial bend point into the arch. The caul should also have a centre line marked on it and have two 8mm holes drilled that line up with the holes drilled for the locating pins.

Another curved caul is useful to clamp over the length of the centre joint. This is made from a piece of 50mm x 50mm wood, a little shorter than the length of the hump, cut to the longitudinal curve of the hump and again faced with cork. This keeps the timber from 'lipping up' as it dries.

Moulding the soundboard

Relatively thick pieces of spruce, around 8mm thick are required. This is much thicker than soundboards usually supplied by most of the tone wood suppliers, so you may have to do a bit of phoning or emailing to find a timber miller who can cut these from a billet of spruce. Thickness the two pieces down to 7mm either with a hand plane, drum sander or thicknesser. Make sure that the inside surfaces are smooth, as when the two haves are moulded and glued together this will become the almost finished inside surface of the soundboard.

All the subsequent thicknessing will be done of the outside. Trim what will be the centre joint so that the grain runs as parallel as possible to what will be the jointed edges. Leave the spruce as rectangular pieces, as this makes gluing the two halves together easier later and drill two 10mm holes that line up with the two locating pins. These are made larger than the pins as the timber will shrink as it dries and move away from the centre line. A loose fit for these holes will preclude any chance of splitting around the holes. A couple of big pencil marks across the outside faces will assist in aligning the two halves at the clamping stage, and I write 'OUT' in big letters as well.

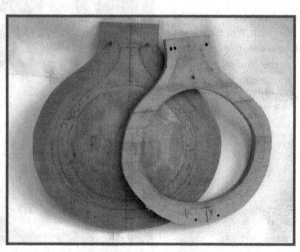

The mould and clamping caul

Soak both halves of the wood in water for at least 24-48 hours. If you have some way of getting them into continuously hot or boiling water this time would probably be reduced, but cold water seems to work fine. After soaking, seal each piece into oven bag material. Ordinary masking tape will seal the bags effectively enough, and the bags need to be fairly tight around the wood. Put the masking tape on what will be the outside surfaces. The bags should be well sealed so that the oven doesn't boil the moisture out of the wood, because it isn't nearly as flexible when that happens. Place the two bags in the oven on its lowest setting, usually about 150°C, and leave for about 20 minutes or until the bags have swollen up from the steam, and the wood feels flexible. Gloves are useful at this stage.

Have the mould, the caul and 8-10 big clamps ready on the bench next to the oven. (Some domestic negotiation may be necessary at this point!) Remove the two pieces of wood from the oven, still in their bags, and align them on the centre line of the mould so they butt together, making sure that the pencil marks on the outside surface of the boards also line up.

Punch the locating pins through the over bags. Place the caul on top and clamp at the neck end, and then another at the tailblock end and then place more clamps around the caul to clamp it firmly down to the mould all the way around. This all has to be done fairly quickly while the wood is still flexible from the heat.

Wait until the whole thing cools down and at this point cut away as much of the bags as is feasible without disturbing the caul and clamp on the secondary longitudinal caul. The next day it can be disassembled, the remnants of the bags removed and then reclamped until fully dry. Leave the whole thing to dry for at least four or five days in a warm spot. Don't try to dry it too quickly by placing it in the sun or over a heating vent. Let it dry slowly so that the tensions in the wood can relax. The spruce will shrink appreciably across its width, with a gap of 2-3mm at each end and more in the centre. When finally disassembled there always is some springback, but there should be close to 15mm of inside arch. If not soak and repeat.

Joining the soundboard

halves

Use a double sided shooting board and a long jack plane to joint the edges as this allows the plane to travel with the grain on both sides of the soundboard. Clamp the flat sections on each end down to the shooting board to make sure everything will be lined up at the gluing stage. A really straight cutting edge on the plane blade is important as different areas of the blade will be cutting the jointed edge because of the arch. More will have to taken off each end to get a straight joint because the arching process leaves a curved edge to the wood. Jim Williams' method of using of an aluminium level with sandpaper glued on one side is a good way if finishing off the joint if a long plane is not available. (see Jim's book *A Guitar Maker's Manual* - Hal Leonard Publications)

The traditional Spanish method of

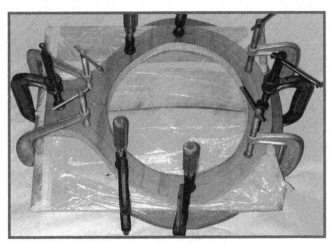

Soundboard halves in the mould

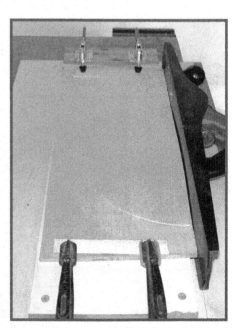

Jointing one moulded half on the double-sided shooting board

50x25mm timber bars, rope and wedges is used to clamp the two halves together, but leaving the top bar off in the centre and using the centre wedge to just push the centre of the joint together if required. After gluing, roping and wedging make sure that the inside edges of the soundboard are as aligned as possible, pushing them into place as necessary.

Carving the soundboard

After letting the centre-joint dry overnight, cut out the shape of the soundboard leaving 1-2mm or so outside the body outline. The different between this method and the usual carving from a sold piece of timber is that in this case the inside arch is already established, and little should need to be done with it. The moisture from the moulding process will have raised the grain along the annular rings and this should be sanded smooth with 120 grit paper. Also smooth any discontinuity on the inside of the join and remove any glue squeezeout. At this point this soundboard had strong #5 mode resonance at C#.

The soundboard is graduated in much

the same way as an archtop guitar or mandolin. The finished thickness will be 5.5mm or a little more in the centre down to 2.5-3mm in the channel 15mm in from the edge with the edge 4.5-5mm thick. The area above the soundhole should remain the same thickness as the edge, with the channel inside the edge disappearing each side of the soundhole.

This graduating can be done quite quickly by depth drilling in concentric circles (turning a little egg-shaped towards the neck) to give thicknesses as appropriate points and then carving and planing away the excess. The initial drilling should be .5mm shallower than the finished thickness. Start by establishing the edge thickness by depth drilling and cleaning up with the small violin makers plane. Using a large gouge (I use 12 and 25mm No 8 sweep and a 18mm No 6 sweep gouge), cutting mostly across the grain, carve the wood away until the drilled holes almost disappear, and then using the two largest Ibex thumb planes, smooth off the gouge marks. Be careful about cutting into the grain runout.

Leave finishing the outside from the

channel to the edge until after the top is glued to the sides so the concavity around the edges can be smooth up to the rim. In any case it is best to cut the channel with the 12mm No.8 gouge. Tap the soundboard again and measure the frequency. At this point the #5 mode frequency was a muddy C with a strong harmonic at F# an octave higher

Using the dial calliper check the thicknesses, marking with a pencil the thickness every 25mm or so over the whole area of the soundboard. Adjust the thickness with gouges and the Ibex planes so the thickness decreases evenly from the centre to the channel. Some archtop and mandolin makers make the graduation more exponential than evenly distributed, with the soundboard thicker for a greater distance from the centre, and this might well work better for softer, lighter spruce.

Tap the soundboard holding it in the lower quarter of the soundboard to hear the #5 mode and check the frequency. The instrument built for this book had a #5 mode resonance at this point of B.

Gluing the moulded soundboard halves together

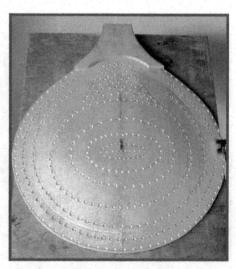

The initial depth drilling

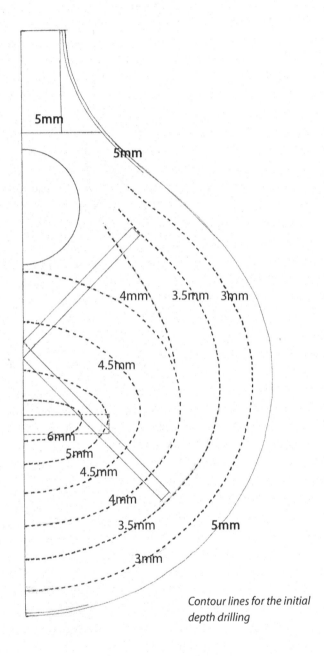

5mm

5mm

4mm   3.5mm   3mm

4.5mm

6mm

5mm

4.5mm

4mm

3.5mm   5mm

3mm

Contour lines for the initial depth drilling

An alternative to a constant 5mm thickness in the area above the soundhole, and the necessity then to fit a fretboard support in that area is laminating two pieces of soundboard offcut (preferably from immediately in front of that section of the soundboard) onto the main soundboard and carving that into a support for the overhanging fingerboard. If fitted carefully the laminated pieces will be virtually invisible after carving. The back edge, immediately in front of the soundhole is sanded to a matching curve to suit the outside diameter of the rosette. The rest of the soundboard can be thicknessed, but leaving the area around the fingerboard until the soundboard is attached to the sides. The angle for the top surface, which will support the fretboard will have to be worked out from a side view diagram. A straight edge along that surface should be 10mm (3/8") above the the bridge position

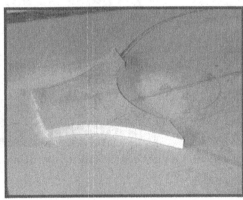

Laminating the fingerboard support. It is located with two small wooden pins - toothpicks or kebab skewers

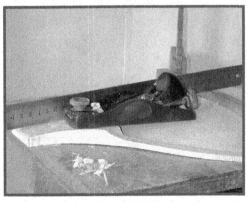

Planing the fingerboard/neck angle

As mentioned in the previous chapter, there are any number of ways that the soundhole rosette can be made. Classical guitars use a complex construction of mosaic tiles and veneer rings, while most steel string guitars use one or more concentric rings of various purflings. There is no reason not to have an oval soundhole, such as the style-4 Gibson mandolin family instruments, f-holes or more fanciful shapes, but I have only built bouzoukis and citterns with round soundholes.

My preferred style is a solid 10mm wide ring of either the same material as the body or the bindings, with the grain going across the soundboard, with the inside of the ring the edge of the soundhole, and purflings on the outside that match those around the soundboard. Feel free to be as inventive as you wish.

The neck edge of the soundhole should be 80mm from the end of the body. This allows 70mm for the heel-less neck mortice with another 10mm clear away from the soundhole edge. This also allows 22 frets clear of the soundhole while allowing the possibility of another 2 frets on a fingerboard extension.

Mark the centre of the soundhole another 40mm away and drill to suit the circle cutter's centre pin. A matching hole is cut in the rectangular workboard which will allow the circle cutter to rotate and be held securely.

A 110-120mm square piece of 2mm thick timber for the rosette should be glued to

Initial carving to the depth of the holes

Checking and marking the thickness with a dial caliper

Smoothing with a violin makers plane

a slightly larger piece of ply or MDF with a drop of glue in the centre. When dry drill a hole for the circle cutter and mount the circle cutter in the drill press on a slow (350 rpm or less) rotational speed. Cut out a circle with a 50mm outside radius and a 40mm inside radius. Cut the outside first and then move it inwards to cut the ring free.

Check the finished diameter of the rosette ring, and mark the inside diameter on the soundboard as well as the outside diameter, plus whatever purflings you want to use. Fit the circle cutter through the hole in the soundboard and the matching hole in the workboard and clamp the soundboard in place. Cut a circle on the inside mark around 2mm deep. Check that the ring just sits outside the inner cut and repeat for the outside circle cut.

Because of the arch in the soundboard it is trickier to cut than on a flat soundboard,

but working away from the centreline gradually from top and bottom of the hole while adjusting the cutter in the slot will realise a smooth, even cut. A few more cuts between the two outside cuts will make chiselling out the waste to a constant depth of 2mm rather easier. Keep in mind the grain runout and be careful not to let the chisel slip and cut into the outside of the channel.

This a job which could be done with a small laminate trimming router or a Dremel in a jig which allowed the router to rise up and down indexed on a foot which remained outside the area to be removed, but I have never got around to making one.

Check the fit of the wood ring and the purflings. They want to be a press fit in to the channel. If the channel is too small use the cutter to slightly enlarge it. If it is too big you will have to rethink the purfling and possibly add a strip to fill the channel. Unclamp the soundboard from the workboard. Glue the rosette in place, with minimal glue to minimise squeezeout, using as many cam clamps as can fit with a piece of clingwrap to stop the clamps

sticking to the rosette. The rosette has to be forced into the transverse arch of the soundboard.

Leave to dry overnight and remove the excess of the rosette down to the level of the soundboard with a scraper and chisels, being careful not to cut into the surrounding spruce. Finish off with small sanding block.

With the soundboard clamped to the workboard again, cut out the soundhole with the circle cutter. Cut most of the way through from the outside and then turn the soundboard over and complete the cut from the inside.

With 120 grit sandpaper slightly round over the inside of the soundhole and clean up any glue around the inside of the rosette.

Again tap the soundboard and note down the frequency or note that results. This one was between A# and B.

The soundboard X-brace

The bridge is 120mm wide, and each

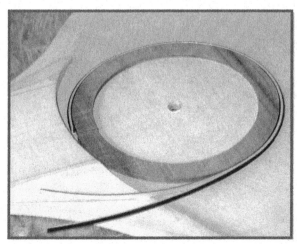
Fitting the purfling strips

The finished rosette

half of the X-brace needs to sit under the edges of the bridge. The upper ends of the braces should not come any closer than 10mm to the edge of the soundhole. Clamp the soundboard face down on the moulding caul with a cam clamp on each side and one each at the top and bottom. It needs to be flat - as it will be when glued to the sides - when fitting the braces. The tendency of the moulded soundboards, because they have been moulded into a complex three-dimensional shape, is for the edges at the widest point of each half to follow the curve in the middle. By the time the graduating is done it is flexible enough to be clamped flat.

Draw the position and outline of the bridge on the inside of the soundboard as well the position of the braces, as per the diagram. The braces are made of 8mm x 20mm brace stock and should end 40mm from the outline on the back edge of the soundboard and 35mm from the outline at the front.

Cut the two braces to length and mark the top end of each one with a number (1 & 2 for simplicity's sake). Trace the curvature of the soundboard onto each brace with a short stub of pencil and cut the marked area away with a chisel or sand it off. This will need to be done a few times until the brace is roughly in contact with the inside of the soundboard along it's whole length. The bottom of the brace will be need to be curved in two directions to fit the contours of the soundboard, rather like a twisted ribbon so it touches along it's entire length, and width.

Place a strip of carbon paper, or ordinary paper rubbed with chalk on the soundboard over the pencil marks and rub the brace back a forward a couple of milimetres. Chisel away the places where the carbon or chalk has marked and repeat until the braces sit fully on the soundboard. Make sure the brace is held upright, and not tilted over. Remove the soundboard from the moulding caul.

Mark the crossing point of each brace and cut notches that are 7.5mm from the soundboard surface. The finished braces will be 15mm at this point, hence the 7.5mm notch. Check the fit of the braces on the soundboard when notched together. Glue the first brace (the one with the notch facing upwards!) in position, holding at each end with a cam clamp and then add other clamps along the length. Clean up any squeezeout.

Leave it for an hour to dry and repeat for the second brace, putting a couple of drops of glue into the notch before fitting. Leave that overnight to dry. Tap the soundboard again. The frequency will have risen, this one up to C#. This will be too high a pitch, and the braces will have to be carved down.

Clamp the soundboard back in the moulding caul again, and carve away the area around the crossing point to 15mm high, and then taper the rest of the braces to 3mm at each end, following the curve of the soundboard.

Tap and measure again. The final note on this instrument was B, but a range of A to C should be fine. If still to high scollop out

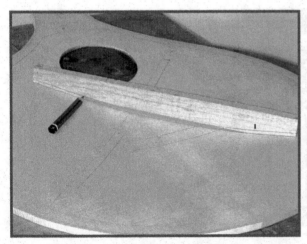

Tracing the soundboard courve onto the brace

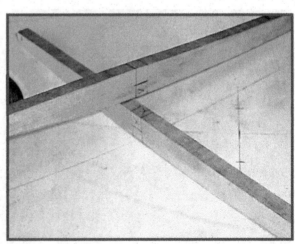

Marking the crossing point

2-3mm between the crossing point and the bridge position and taper the tops of the braces to a point.

These braces are not so much supporting the soundboard and the string tension as controlling the soundboard resonances. These resonances will change quite radically when the soundboard is glued to the sides, and then again when the final carving is done around the edges.

The soundboard can now be glued to the sides and block assembly.

When making any instrument, it is good practice to write down the tap tones at progressive stages of soundboard construction. After listening to the finished instrument and noting where the tap tones occured, it becomes possible after a few instruments to start to to control the sound by controlling the tap tones. It is a mix of art, science and intuition, but it does help.

With 7mm Englemann spruce moulded, glued up and cut to shape, there was a strong resonance between C and C#.

Carved to 6.5mm in the centre and a little over 3mm in the channel, with edges at 5.5mm there was a resonance at C an octave higher and another strong one at F# (another one of those mysterious things which I don't really understand). With the soundboard carved and sanded down to 5.5mm in the centre and 3mm in the channel the note dropped to B. Cutting the soundhole dropped the note again to between B and A# and when 8 x 15mm X braces were glued on it rose again to C# an octave higher.

Profiling the braces brought this down to between C and C# and carving the braces down to 3mm high at each end dropped the note to B.

With the top glued to the sides and the headblock fingerbraces glued the note went up again to G#, with the edges still

a little thick and a 10-12mm wide area between the channel and the binding still too thick. When the back was glued on the air resonance was a little above C and when final carving and sanding was completed the air resonance was right between C# and D, which stayed much the same after lacquering.

Again, these frequencies were within the expected ranges that other similar instruments have exhibited. The critical factor is the resonance of the free plate before it is glued to the sides. Somewhere between A and B is optimal. I built one moulded top arch-top which was entirely too stiff, with a free plate resonance of D. It exhibited lots of unpleasant overtones and I eventually replaced the top, which improved it dramatically.

Gluing the soundboard braces

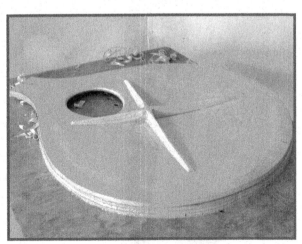

The inside of the finished soundboard

The process here is essentially the same as carving a mandolin or arch-top guitar soundboard. The outside of the soundboard is carved first, and then the inside is hollowed out, leaving the centre of the soundboard around 6mm thick, tapering to 2.5-3mm thick in the re-curve 15mm in from the edges and then thickening to a 5mm thick edge. The major difference is the way I do the area above the soundhole, carved to support the fingerboard (using a bolt-on mortice and tenon neck with a heel) or to give a visual effect of bring the soundboard up to the bottom of the fingerboard (using a heel-less neck and similar to the technique described in the chapter on moulded arch-top soundboards)

Arching height

Mandolin soundboards typically have an arching height of around 15mm, while Robert Bennedetto carves his arch-top guitars to around 22mm, measured from the bottom of the soundboard to the highest outside point of the arch. The soundboard illustrated here is for an 18.5" scale mandola, which is a bouzouki scaled down from 350 to 315 wide. It uses a 17mm arching height, while a bouzouki would use an arching height of 19-20mm.

Whether for a mandolin or a guitar the carved thicknesses remain much the same - around 6mm /.250" in the centre, down to 3mm/.125" or a little less for a mandolin, in the recurve channel inside the edge.

Making the carving templates

The most effective way to end up with the outside of the soundboard the right shape is to use templates. The next page has a diagram showing the layout. but it is a simple process to create your own arching templates.

Draw a half body outline on a sheet of card, with the centreline 50-60mm in from an edge. This gives enough room to draw the longitudinal arch. Mark the bridge position and the finished arch height on the opposite side of the centreline to the body outline. Mark a point 10mm above the arching height, which will be the theoretical extension of a line along the bottom of the fingerboard. At the neck end of the body mark 8mm above the centreline, which will be the bottom of the fingerboard at that point (note that this is 3mm above the edges around the rest of the body, and the edges will flare up to that point.)

Laying out the arching templates

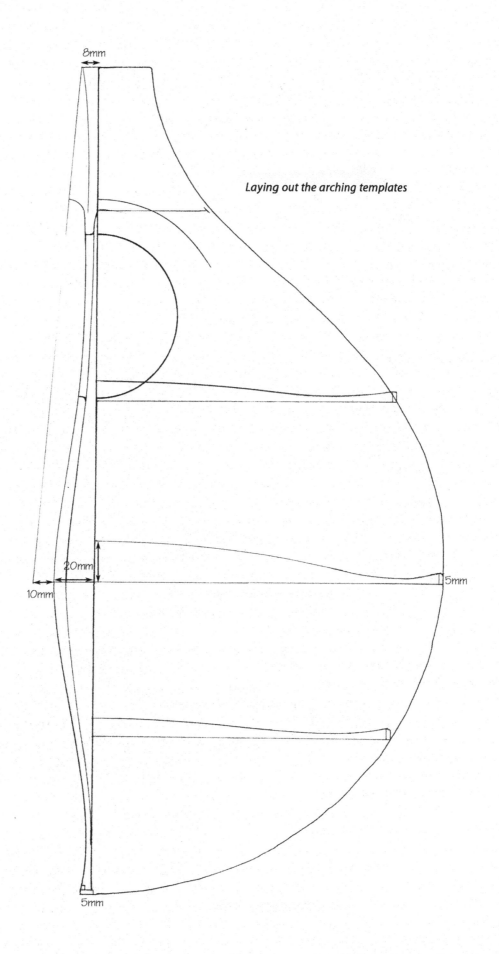

8mm

Laying out the arching templates

20mm

10mm

5mm

5mm

The thinnest point of the soundboard is 3mm in the recurve channel 15mm in from the edge. Mark that point and join up the points using a flexible curve or similar. This is the centreline arching.

The transverse templates are made in a similar way by drawing curves based on the centre arching height and the recurve and edges. Trace or photocopy the template shapes and cut them out of card. If carving the soundboard with the fingerboard extension support it is worthwhile making two centreline templates, one without the fingerboard support which makes it easier to carve the rest first.

The Soundboard Blank

A carved bouzouki/cittern soundboard will need two pieces of book-matched timber 450mm x 180mm x 25mm This is larger than most mandolin blanks. but a lot smaller than a guitar. Ask your wood supplier for a suitably sized block.

The centre joint has to be precise, as for any other centreboard join, but more difficult to achieve because the wood is thicker. A very important first step is to get the bottom surface of each side flat, without any winding.

An 8″ jointer is a really quick way to do this, but it may be down to a plane and sanding boards if a big jointer isn't available. Just make sure, if using wedges split from a billet, that the thinnest part is still at least 6mm (1/4″).

Once the flat bottom surface is established the centreline join can be prepared square to the bottom surface. Again, a well set up jointer is a good way to cut this joint, but a shooting plane and a sanding board (as described in the moulded archtop chapter) can be used.

Two or three sash clamps, pipe clamps or similar will be needed. If the soundboard halves were cut from a wedge, they will be thinner towards the edges, and this can make clamping a tricky process, with the clamping pressure not centred on the joint. Two clamps under and one over helps here as will a dry run before applying any glue. This has to be a tight joint. Let the glue dry overnight.

Establishing the edge thickness

Planing the fingerboard support angle

Initial Shaping of the Soundboard

Reduce the overall thickness of the soundboard down to just over (less than 1mm) the finished arching height using a thicknessing sander or a hand plane. Trace out the body outline from the half body template and cut out the shape on a bandsaw. It is best to check the outline on the side assembly for any difference between the template shape and the side outline. Trim the soundboard edges down to within 1mm of the finished size. A combination of disc sander and drum sanders will do this quickly and efficiently.

Mark the position of the soundhole and the fingerboard extension. If the neck end of the soundboard is to be carved to support the fingerboard, mark the position of the end of this. The photographs will show the shape of this area.

The edges of the soundboard should be reduced to a little over 5mm (3/16") all around except for the areas above the top edge of the soundhole. This should extend 15mm (5/8") in from the edge. Using the centreline template start carving the longitudinal arch. A 25mm (1") gouge is the best tool for the initial hogging off. Leave the fingerboard support section alone at this time, but carve away the area below it where the soundhole will be cut, starting to form the curved wings around the soundhole. A smaller gouge 10-12mm wide is useful here.

Once the general shape of the longitudinal arch is formed, start on the transverse arching using the three templates. Carve three transverse strips to shape and then carve away the areas in between. By now the soundboard should be starting to look something like a carved soundboard .

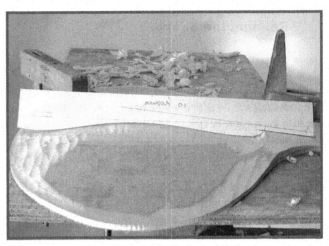

Carving the the lengthways arch

Finishing the preliminary carving

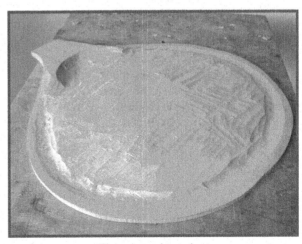

The recurve channel cut

Refining the Shape

Use a small curved sole violin makers plane to smooth away the gouge marks, checking with the templates. The templates will still be sitting a little high, because the recurve has yet to be carved. This is the thinnest part of the soundboard at 3mm (.125") at this stage of carving and 15mm (5/8") in from the edge. Use a depth drill setup on the drill press to 3.5mm (.140") and drill around a line 15mm in from the edge up to a point in line with the middle of the soundhole. Carve the recurve channel leaving a 5mm of flat at the edges and blend in the inside into the arching which will have to be adjusted to fit the templates into the recurve.

The fingerboard support can now be planed to the correct angle. I make the soundboard 8mm (5/16") thick at the neck join, rather than the 5mm for the rest of the edges. The arching template will give a close approximation of the correct angle, but the critical part is to keep this area flat laterally and a straight edge laid lengthways should project 10mm (3/8") above the soundboard at the bridge position.

The wing extensions around the top edge of the rosette and the flaring up of the edges to the neck join can now be roughed out, but final carving is best left until the soundboard is glued to the side assembly and the neck fitted.

Sand with 80 grit paper to get rid of the gouge/plane marks and check for lateral symmetrically. The curves should be smooth, especially when the curves change from from convex to concave.

The recurve channel cut and getting close to the final shape

Checking the shape against the centre transverse template

The preliminary depth drilling on the inside

Hollowing the Inside

Set up the depth drilling jig on the drill press for slightly over a 6mm (1/4") depth and drill the inside of the soundboard at close intervals with a 5mm (3/16") bit. The more that is drilled out, the less has to be carved away.

Carve out the drilled area until the bottoms of the holes are just disappearing. This is a half hour's job with a sharp gouge or a couple of minutes with carving attachment on an angle grinder. Quick but scary, as it is all to easy to cut too much away

Once the initial 6mm thickness is established, a second drilling is done to indicate what will be close to the final thicknessing. For this I use a small ball burr that came with a Dremel kit, but a drill bit is fine. Concentric oval shapes (as on the diagram on page 61) at .5mm (.020") intervals of thickness will give a good reference for the removal of the wood. It gets a bit more complex around the top end of the soundboard, but the soundboard should be around 4-4.5mm thick in the area where the soundhole will be cut. It is best to drill a little thicker than the finished thickness. Remove the wood with a gouge until the bottoms of the holes are just showing and then smooth away with a small violin makers plane.

Check the thicknesses with a dial calliper, marking with pencil and adjust with the place or scraper until correct. Final thicknesses will depend on the piece of wood used, but a centre thickness of 6mm (.250") and 2.5-3mm (.100-.120") in the channel is a good start.

This mandola soundboard tap toned at G# which is about right for an instrument with a low C string. The air resonance of the finshed instrument was just below F.

Soundhole cutting and bracing can be done in the same way as described in the chapter on moulded arch-tops.

The preliminary inside drilling carved out

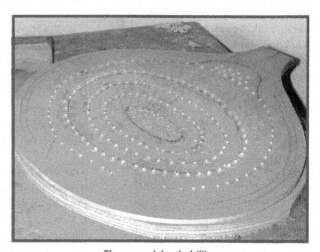

The second depth drilling

The thickness marked on the inside after carving

Like a flat-top soundboard the back is made from two (or occasionally more) bookmatched pieces of the same timber as the sides. In a perfect world the back would be cut from the same block of wood as the sides, but often it is a matter of matching up grain and colour to be as similar as possible. This doesn't usually matter so much with mahogany, but there can be a lot of variation in the various rosewoods and other woods such as Tasmanian blackwood (black acacia). Most tonewood supplier will endeavour to sell back and side sets matched in colour and grain. At the very least, the two halves of the back should be sawn sequentially from one plank, as should the two sides (but perhaps not the same plank)

Joining and Thicknessing the Back

Hold the two haves together and look at the endgrain and sawmarks along the sides to establish in which order they were sawn. Open the two pieces out like a book and lay them side by side on the workbench and establish which is the most attractive match of grain down the centrejoin. If it is a flamed or figured timber the edges with the most flame or figure should be in the centre. If the grain doesn't run parallel to the proposed centrejoin the two halves can be trimmed, or the 'arrowhead' pattern should point towards the neck.

Mark the edges to be joined with a pencil and join the two halves in the same way as the flat-top soundboard. Let the glue dry overnight and thickness the back to 2.5mm thick. This can be hard work on a rosewood or figured Tasmanian blackwood, so a thickness sander is preferred, but not essential.

If thicknessing with a hand plane, smooth the outside surface first and sand smooth. Until the outside is smooth only plane the inside surface to level any major differences in thickness. Once finished draw a centreline down the inside of the back.

Many guitar makers inlay a decorative centrestrip on the outside of the back join. This often matches the bindings or can be a contrasting marquetry strip. A slot can be cut out with an appropriate router bit to half the back thickness, and the strip glued in before final thicknessing. I don't use them, but there is no reason not to.

My colleague Graham Caldersmith, who has done extensive experimental work with guitars, suggests that there are advantages to be had with a back as stiff as possible as this can minimise the interaction between air moving in the soundhole and the fundamental soundboard resonance. Caldersmith has made his classical guitar backs around 5mm (3/16") thick and Greg Smallman's guitars use a moulded and arched laminated back which is very stiff.

My preference is towards lightness in construction wherever possible, but stiffening a back plate through stiffer braces might well have advantages

Gluing the back centre reinforcement strip

The Backstrip

Cut the back out to 3mm outside the body outline. Place the side/block assembly on the inside of the back, keeping the centrelines of both aligned, and trace around the blocks and linings.

The backstrip is a 2-3mm thick x 18mm wide piece of wood with the grain running a right angles to the centre line that is glued on the inside of the back to re-enforce the back centre join. The simplest way to make such a strip is to cut it from one end of a thicknessed flat-top soundboard. A bouzouki/cittern body is usually shorter than the guitar sized soundboard halves bought from the supplier, so there should be enough spare for the backstrip. Sand the edges smooth with a halfsheet sanding block or a beltsander, being careful not to break it as it will break along the grain (which runs across it's width) rather easily.

Cut it long enough to it overlaps the pencilled marks for the endblock, and mark with a pencil the outside at both ends. Run a thin smear of glue over the whole of one side and clamp it in place. Preferably glue it using the 15' radius dished workboard with go-sticks, using thin, but flexible strips to protect it from the ends of the go-sticks. This isn't essential, but every bit of assistance to form the back into the section of a 15' radius sphere is helpful.

This and subsequent gluing procedures should be done at humidity levels of 40-45%

Unclamp it after an hour and taper the sides of the strip down to almost nothing with a chisel, and sand to a smooth curve with 120 grit paper.

The Back Braces

For many years I used three transverse braces, sanded to a 15' radius curve, which set the transverse curve of the back, but did little to establish the longitudinal curve necessary to fit the back. The idea of transverse back braces goes back to the days before soundboard fan or X bracing, and is one of those things that is done because it has always been done. In recent years a number of builders have started using a X brace for the back, and Al Carruth, writing in *American Lutherie* No 30 (Summer 1992), puts forward some good reasons for using an X brace on the back as a way of controlling the back resonances in relation to the top resonances. If nothing else, X bracing the back puts in the required longitudinal curve to help fit the back and that is good.

Gluing the back X-braces

The X brace shaped

The back braces can be made from quarter sawn spruce, or mahogany if you wish, with the annual rings running vertical to the back. Two pieces 8x15mm by 360mm are needed with a 15' radius curve on one of the 8mm wide sides. The plans in the back of the book have a template for this curve. A disk sander or router table jig is the quickest way to accurately shape the braces to shape, but it can be done with a block plane, being careful to keep the curved side square to the sides of the brace.

The crossing point of the X should happen around the widest point of the body, which should be close to the bridge position on the soundboard. Use a long straight edge with a protractor and pencil to mark to position of the X braces, using a 90° or a little greater angle between them. Cut the notches in the same way as described in the chapters on soundboards. The centrestrip will need to be cut away at the crossing point for the braces to fit. Cut at the pencil marks with a chisel or knife and use a 1/4" chisel to remove the waste. Check the fit.

The back braces should extend under the linings, with notches cut out of the linings to fit. This is useful when fitting the back, as the notches will stop the back sliding around on the wet glue. Some builders extend the tapered ends of the braces right through the sides, covering them with the bindings, or they can be stopped just inside the sides, but still under the linings. In either case trim them to a length which just overlaps the outside of the body and glue in place, preferably using the 15' radius dished workboard and go-sticks, although long clamps can be used. Make sure the entire bottom (curved) surface is lightly coated with glue. Clean up any squeezeout with a scrap of wood, card or a plastic drinking straw cut at an angle.

Shaping the back braces

The end 40mm of the braces should be scalloped down to disappear just inside the sides. The rest of the braces should be profiled to a pointed shape with a chisel and sanded smooth to 120 grit. The crossing point of the X can be left square or the pointed profiles continued until they meet at the intersection.

Fitting the back

With the back laid on the workboard, place the side assembly on top, lining up the centrelines and making sure there is a roughly equal overlap of the back. Trace around the outside of the sides with a pencil, mark where the back centrestrip has to be trimmed and mark the positions of the back braces on the linings. Remove the side assembly and trim the ends of the braces if necessary. With a fine saw and a 1/4" chisel cut tapered mortices in the lining to accept the ends of the braces. Trim the centrestrip to length with a chisel and set the back aside until the soundboard is glued onto the sides.

This chapter deals with gluing together the various subassemblies - the soundboard, the sides and the back, and then fitting the heel-less neck. The trickiest part is getting the body mortice on an arch-top body at the correct angle. This can be done by hand or with a fairly complex jig.

Attaching a flat-top soundboard

The area around the edge of the soundboard, from the soundhole back needs to be supported to allow for the slight arch built in from the braces. A couple of layers of card in a crescent shape is all that is necessary. Line up the centreline drawn on the inside of the soundboard with the centreline of the workboard and hold it in place with the soundhole clamp (described in the section on jigs). Place the side assembly on the soundboard, lining up the centrelines drawn on the neck and tailblocks and check that the main X braces clear the linings. They should taper to nothing just before the linings, but they can continue into the linings if you wish (cut slots to fit, but stop them just before the sides). Check that the centrelines on the soundboard and both blocks line up and when everything is correct run a bead a glue around all the gluing surfaces of the side assembly and clamp it in place. Start with the end blocks and add three or four around the sides. Clean up any squeezeout with plastic straw or scrap of wood and let dry overnight. Remove the soundboard clamp. If this is not done before gluing on the back, you are in big trouble.

Attaching an archtop soundboard

A spacer is needed to keep the top of the arch clear of the workboard. A shaped form similar to that used as the clamping caul for moulding the soundboard is necessary, but with the outside the same as the body and 12mm wide except for the area around the neck block which should be the same size as that block. Otherwise proceed as before unless a laminated fingerboard support has been added. In this case a wedge needs to be made to support the angled face.

If using a solid headblock and a neck with a heel, the neck needs to be fitted at this point as described in Chapter 6.

The soundhole braces

Because of the shape of the instrument the stress of the neck under string tension will always want to rotate the neck block back in a way that does not happen as much in guitars. Two 6 x 6mm braces should run from either side of the end of the neck out to meet the X-braces. This helps stop any tendency for the soundboard to buckle around the top of the soundhole, which is a common problem in many old mandolins.

Gluing the soundboard to the sides

These small braces should butt up tightly to the neck block and X- brace and be clamped in place with a small G clamp through the soundhole, with a caul to protect the outside of the soundboard.

This is a good time to have another listen to the soundboard tap-tones. It will have gone up in pitch from the free-plate tap-tone, but there is some thinning to be done yet. Tap the soundboard in the centre and note down the pitch.

Gluing the back

Make sure there are centrelines on each end of the body which you can match up to the centreline of the back, which should be the centre glue joint unless you have used a three-piece back. Make the centreline of the back plainly visible on the endgrain of the back plate, and check for fit, making sure the centrestrip isn't squashed under either of the blocks and the braces fit into the notches cut for them in the linings.

Run a bead of glue over all the gluing surfaces on the side assembly, smoothing it off over the neck block and clamp the back in place with large rubber bands about 150mm (6") long and 12mm (1/2") wide. A cam clamp or two at each end can be useful. The rubber bands will go around the slots cut in the workboard for positioning the side dowels. Use as many as you need to hold the back evenly on the sides. The glue joint between the back and the neck block is critical so make sure this is firmly clamped across the whole area. Leave to dry overnight

Trimming the soundboard and back and sanding

Before the binding rebates can be cut the overhang of the soundboard and back must be trimmed back flush with the sides. This can be done with a chisel or with a router. The router can be set up with a 1/2" ball bearing flush trimming bit or with the 1/4" spiral bit and the routing guide set so it cuts flush. In either case it is best to cut away the overhang at the widest point of the body first, where the soundboard grain runs almost parallel to the sides, as this has a tendency to be torn out by the router.

The sides need to be sanded to remove any ripples or lumpy bits of bending, as the guide for the binding channels must run along the sides and any imperfections there will get transferred to the binding channel. This can be done with a sanding block and 80 grit paper or with a sanding drum mounted in the drill press. Be careful not to sand the sides too thin - under 1.5mm. It is better to have a slight imperfection in the side curve than to have the side too thin and fragile.

The flat-top soundboard edges should be thinned down at this stage. From around 35-40mm in from the sides from the bottom of the soundhole back the soundboard thickness should be reduced gradually down to 2mm at the edges. Use a sharp plane set very fine and keep in mind the direction of the runout, especially around the centre joint. Sand smooth with the half sheet block faced with 120 grit paper or an orbital sander with a medium (120 grit) disc.

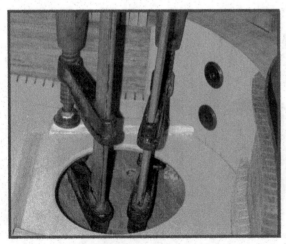

Clamping the soundhole braces

The back glued with rubber bands

I don't know of many makers who enjoy binding instruments. It has to be done quite meticulously and any errors are tricky to hide. It is quite possible to do the whole job with a purfling cutter, which can be simply made, and a couple of small chisels, but it is hard work through a timber like rosewood. The most common method is to use a router with a guide system to hold the router parallel to the sides and to control the depth of the cut. These can be very simple as shown in the picture on the next page or much more complex with screw adjustments for width and depth.

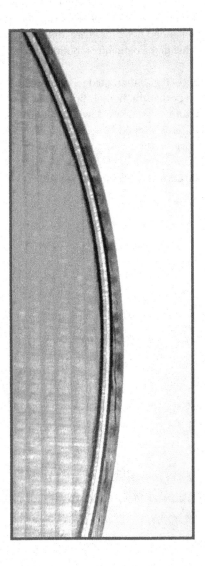

The body should be able to be held with clamps so that the router can be run around the edges of the instrument. Four small L shaped supports that sit in the workboard slots and a cam clamp will work well. The ultimate approach to a binding jig is one that holds the instrument body, rotates it while holding the router at an infinitely variable position through a set of articulated joints. Gilet Guitars in Sydney have been working on such a jig for some years and reckon they have the problem fixed.

A purfling cutter, whether shop built or a commercially made, is still useful when cutting the binding and purfling channels with a router as a scribe with the cutter before routing can help with avoiding chipping on the bottom edges of the channels.

The role of the binding is both protective and decorative. Around the soundboard it protects the endgrain of the spruce and is usually made from a harder material than the soundboard so it can take the inevitable dings on the corners of the edges. Binding of a contrasting colour can also provide an attractive 'frame' to set off the shape of the instrument.

If there is ever a need for major surgery on the instrument body the bindings can be cut away to allow access to the soundboard or back joint and then replaced fully after the work has been done, but you have to hope this never has to happen.

Binding is usually either timber or celluloid which is available in white, black, a cream/ivory colour or tortoiseshell. Both wooden and celluloid bindings can be purchased from lutherie suppliers, the wooden ones sometimes with a contrasting strip on the bottom edge. Cellulloid binding have the advantage of not having to be bent to shape, but do need a special acrylic cement, the stype used for gluing perspex. Alternatively wooden bindings can be made from offcuts of the sides, which usually come rather wider as raw stock from a supplier than is needed for a bouzouki.

While the sides are thicknessed to 2mm, I leave the bindings at 2.5mm, but that is an individual decision and 2mm bindings are fine too. A 5mm binding height suits the proportion if the body, but it can be a little higher, especially if you want to cover the soundboard-side join on an archtop model where the soundboard will be 4.5-5mm thick.

The assembly workboard with the body support shoes.

Purflings are coloured strips of wood or sometimes plastic which form a decorative line inside the bindings. They are most often in combinations of black and white strips as well as geometric patterns like the famous Martin herringbone. A black/white or black/white/black is commonly used around the soundboard, with the option to do the same, or perhaps a pattern slightly simpler inside the bindingss on the back.

Making wooden bindings

They can be thicknessed in the same way as the sides, with with a plane and scrapers or a thicknessing sander. It is easier to do this in wider strips and then cut to final width. A round nosed fence on the bandsaw can be used, but plane one edge of the binding strip first and the rough sawn edge can be left until after the binding is glued in place. A shooting plane can be held upside down in a vice and the strip pulled across to true up the edges.

Wooden binding needs to be bent to the body outline, and this can be on the same heated mold used for the sides or by hand over a hot pipe. If 2mm thick binding are used, they can be bent at the same time as the sides on the heated mold, held in place with masking tape.

The thicker bindings should be bent sparately, but can be done four at a time, again held together with masking tape at each end and the middle. The most important part of the bending is the concave curve around the neck block and the transition into the convex curve around the rest of the body. This needs to sit exactly into the binding rebate, otherwise it is very hard to avoid an unsightly gap. If the bindings have been left rough on one edge remember that they must be bent with two in a mirror image to the other two, so the finished edge sits in the bottom of the channelt.

Cutting the binding channels

With the purfing cutter set to the required finished depth of the bindings scribe a line around the sides. This will help to minimise chipping along the bottom of the channel. You can use the cutter and a chisel to do the whole job, of course, but otherwise it is time for the router. The drawing in the jigs section shows the fence which must be made for the router to keep the router bit vertical and to cut an even channel.

Use a solid carbide 1/4" down cut spiral bit which will last for between 6-10 instruments. Once it gets blunt it starts to tear bits of wood out along the bottom of the slot and to fuzz up the endgrain of the soundboards.

Have a piece of scrap timber clamped in the vise to check the correct depth and width of the routing. A short length of 100mm x 50mm (4"x2") pine is good. The width of the channel should be a little bit deeper than the width of the binding, just enough to feel with a finger nail. This means that the sides have to be slightly sanded down to meet to bottom edge of the bindings, which will mean a slight convexity to the sides. It is only a few thousandths of an inch or tenths of a millimentre, but it means that the binding will remain at the same thickness and not be thinned out if there are imperfections either in the bending or routing process.

Once the router guide is correctly set check that the body is firmly held in the fixture, soundboard down. Turn the router on, and with the bottom of the guide touching the sides, move it towards the instrument so the top guide is resting on the back and bit is starting to cut.

The binding channel routing jig

A body ready for routing

Keep the bottom of the vertical guide firmly on the sides and don't worry if the router isn't cutting the full width of the channel and the top of the vertical guide isn't flush. It is better to cut the channel in a couple of passes rather than have to push too hard to cut in one pass.

You can, of course, set the router up to cut either a shallower or narrower cut and then re-adjust it to complete the channel. What ever you are comfortable with. In any case do not try to do it too quickly. Take your time and remember that routers are dangerous beasts.

Repeat the process for the top edges. The spruce will tend to fuzz up where the router is cutting into the end grain, and be careful around the widest points of the body as the router can grab a bit of spruce along the grain and rip it out. Clean up the channels with a sharp 1/4" and 3/8" chisel and a square medium cut file. The width of the slot can be checked by eye and test fitted with the binding. Remember the outside of the binding should sit just inside the sides.

If adding a lamination to build up the thickness of an archtop soundboard in the area above the soundhole, the final thickness of the soundboard at the neck join has to be kept in mind. On this instrument the bindings will need to be 8mm high at the neck join, compared to 5mm for the rest of the body and the bindings were cut 9mm wide for the last couple of inches. For dark (eg rosewood) bindings a strip can be glued on top of the main bindings and faired into the soundboard. This will mean that both the binding and purfling channels will have to be cut by hand for the last inch or so and the neck fitted before the bindings and purflings are cut

The router now needs to be re-setup to cut the pufling channel. The channel should be .5mm shallower than the purfling and exactly the width of the purfling inside the binding. Use the piece of scrap 4x2 to get this right and rout the channel. Don't worry about the fuzz as after the puflings are glued into place they can be sanded away.

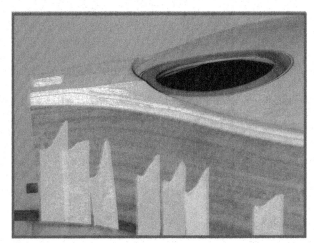

The channel for a fully carved soundboard or a moulded arch-top with the neckblock lamination

A body ready for gluing the binding

The end bindings

It is convention to cover the join at the tail end where the sides meet. It gives a visual tieing together of the back and top bindings as well as covering any slight in accuracy when the sides where trimmed and glued to the tailblock. This can be a simple rectangular strip the same width and material as the bindings, or a tapered wedge. A wedge should taper from 10-12mm at the top to 6mm at the bottom. The centrelines of the the top and back should meet with a vertical line taken from the soundboard, but if not mark a centreline down from the centreline of the soundboard.

Draw the outside edges of the butt-strip and score with a Exacto knife using a short metal straight edge as a guide. Use a 1/4" chisel to cut a angled ledge on the inside and then a fine backsaw to cut the rest of the way through the side material. Remove the waste with the chisel. If using a tapered wedge, cut it over length and check the fit.

The tapered shape means you can adjust the taper until it is a tight fit. Cut it to a couple of millimetres or so longer than is necessary, smear with glue and push it into place. A couple of strips of masking tape will make sure it doesn't move. When the glue is dry carefully trim the butt-strip flush with the bottoms of the binding channels.

This strip can be more decorative than a simple wedge of timber. An alternative is to insert a wedge of the same timber as the sides, with the grain running vertically, and edge it with thin strips of the binding and perhaps even a frame of purfling.

Because the teardrop bouzouki shape ends with a square block where the neck attaches, especially for the heel-less neck, the ends of the front ends of the sides and the front end of the back should also be bound. Again this should be the same size and materials as the rest of the binding and the channels will need to be cut in the same way as the butt-strip. They can be glued in place at this point and trimmed flush with the channels. If a light coloured binding is used it will look better to mitre the strips at the ends of the sides after the main side binding is in place.

Cutting the tapered channel with a knife

Cleaning the channel with a small chisel

Gluing the Bindings

If the back is just being bound without any purfling, take the first bent binding strip and sit it in the channel, making sure that the concave curve around the neck-block lines up. Hold it fairly tightly in place with a couple of strips of masking tape and mark where it meets the middle of the butt-strip. Cut to that length, though you can allow a little extra to make a mitred joint rather than a simple butt joint.

Repeat for the other side making sure the two ends meet squarely at the butt-joint. Trim the neck block end, allowing 10mm overhang. If using a celluloid binding just trim one end of each to a square mitred joint and cut the binding approximately to length. Allow 25mm as an overhang, just to make sure it doesn't end up too short.

For wooden bindings, run a bead of glue along the binding channel on one side from the butt joint to the front end of the body and start taping the binding in place from the butt-strip. The point where the bindings join should be in the centreline of the butt-strip. Hold the binding in place with a thumb and run a strip of masking tape or plastic packing tape from the sides over onto the back, pulling the binding snugly into place. Because the back follows a 15' diametre

radis in all directions the binding channel will not be stright and will curve towards the soundboard along it's length. Towards the neck-block are the binding will need to be pushed down to the bottom of the channel and simultaneously pulled in and taped in place.

It may be necessary to use a cam-clamp to hold the end of the binding strip in place if it wants to spring back too badly. Repeat for the other side, making sure the join at the butt-strip is as tight as possible. If a clamp has been used to hold the binding in place at the neck block end, leave it overnight to dry.

For celluloid binding the same process is used, but it is better to apply the acrylic cement over a shorter length at the time, 100-125mm (4-5"). It should be flexible enough to be able to be pulled into the longitudinal curve of the body without any clamps.

Binding the soundboard is a bit tricker,

as you have to deal with not only the binding, but one or more strips of purfling as well. The purfling strips look better visually if the ends that meet at the tail are mitred, though if there is to be a tailpiece over the top it doesn't matter all that much. Simple black/white pufling will be flexible enough to conform to the body outline. Run a bead of glue into each level of the binding channel of one side of the soundboard as well as on any surface of the binding/purflings which join each other.

Tape the tail end of the strips down over the butt strip, making sure everything is kept together. Add a few more strips of masking tape. The purfling strips will be annoyingly waving around in the air at this point, so tape them loosly to the concave curve around the neck block. This should not be too tight, as all that is necessasary is to keep them out of the way.

Continue taping the binding/purfling

The binding glued and held with masking tape

The neckblock binding on a heel-less neck instrument

strips in place, making sure that the purfling is tight againt the edges of the soundboard, and the binding sits neatly in it's channel. Getting the purfling snug against the soundboard edge is important for the finished look of the instrument and filling in gaps along the purfling is hard and difficult to hide. When finished, repeat for the other side and leave overnight.

If not done previously glue in the butt strip and the binding around the neck block. It looks neater to mitre in the vertical strips along the front ends of the sides, but if a dark binding like Rosewood is used they can be just cut to size to fit between the top and back binding. Hold them in place with more masking tape.

Trimming the bindings

Remove the masking tape and with a block plane/chisel/scraper cut away the top edges of the bindings until they are flush with the soundboard and back. Be careful of the grain direction of the bindings ands finish off with 120 grit paper for the soundboard and 80 grit then 120 grit paper for the back.

If the binding channels were correctly cut, the binding should be sitting just about flush with the sides. Use a stiff scraper to level off any high points on either and sand with 80 grit, then 120 grit paper. Try not to thin down either the bindings or the sides themselves too much.

The edges of the bindings should be rounded over with a scraper and sandpaper. Care should be taken where the back bindings meet the heel of the neck (if built that way) so the chamfer of the bindings and heep cap is continuous.

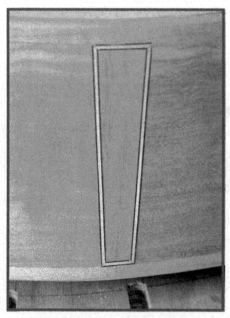

Framing the butt-strip with purfling

Using the binding material to frame the butt strip

This procedure opens up the neck mortice at the end of the body and holes are drilled through to the back of the instrument so the neck attachment bolts can be tightened. A simple jig is required to locate the holes accurately, and if the mortice was not cut when making the hollow neck-block a more complex jig will need to be constructed to accurately route out the mortice.

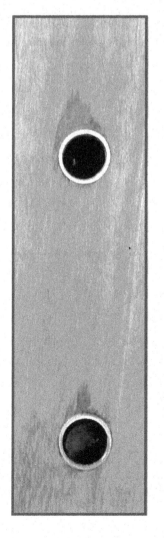

Flat-top fitting

The soundboard over the mortice in the neckblock should be cut away. An Exacto knife will cut through the spruce, and cut to within a millimetre or so of the sides of the mortice. Measure where the end of the mortice will be and cut across along that line (which will probably cut through the top of the rosette) with the knife. Trim the edges to meet the sides of the mortice.

Drilling the neck bolt holes

A drilling guide will be needed to drill holes vertically through the bottom of neck mortice and through to the back of the instrument. A 70mm long and 75mm high block should be made of MDF, or a combination of MDF and plywood that is the same tapered shape as the neck mortice. It needs 1/4" holes drilled in the same position as the T-nuts in the neck.

Clamp the block firmly in the mortice and drill the two back holes with a long 1/4" bit. Don't try to go all the way through the bottom of the neck block at this point. Drop a couple of long 1/4" bolts into the back holes to keep the drilling block positioned, take the clamp off and drill the two front holes in the same way.

Remove the block and drill the holes through the bottom of the neckblock and the back. Place a piece of scrap timber underneath the back to prevent tearout when drilling the holes all the way through.

Depending on what kind of T-nuts were used, 4 x 1" x 1/4" UNC/Whitworth or 4 x 25mm M6 bolts will be needed to attach the neck. The best are machine bolts with an allen key head, which can be tightened through the holes in the back. To finish off the holes in the back glue in short lengths of brass tubing using 5 minute epoxy. The brass tube needs an inner diameter large enough for the required allen key. The holes through the back may need to be enlarged. An alternative is a plate that can be screwed over the access holes made from an off cut of the back material

Drilling the first two neck bolt holes

If all has gone to plan the neck should sit comfortably in the mortice with the bottom of the fretboard in line with the top of the soundboard. If the mortice is too tight (which is better than it being too loose) gradually enlarge it with a chisel until the neck fits. Fit a couple of the bolts and check the neck alignment. Hold a long straight edge held along each side of the neck and draw a line at the bridge position. These should be equidistant from the soundboard centreline. If they are not, the mortice will have to be adjusted, widen at one end or another until correct.

Check the angle of the neck by holding the straight edge along the centre of the fingerboard and checking the height above the soundboard at the bridge position which should be 10mm. If it is less then 9mm the neck should be shimmed by gluing a piece of veneer at the end of the neck block (or the end of the mortice) and if more than 10.5mm the end of the mortice should be deepened a little with a chisel, being careful to keep the bottom of the mortice flat.

Arch-top fitting

This is rather more complex that fitting the neck to a flat-top as the tapered mortice has to be angled down at a precise angle to establish the correct bridge height. The earlier section on making the hollow head block covered cutting a slightly shallow mortice and this now needs to be adjusted to the correct depth and/or angle.

The soundboard over the neckblock mortice should be cut away to open up the mortice. Whether the soundboard has been left at 5mm thick or an extra lamination of timber has been glued on a fine saw and chisels will be needed to remove it. Be careful to keep the sides vertical. Once the mortice is opened up check for lengthways alignment as described previously and adjust the width and taper if necessary to get the neck centred on the body centreline and the appropriate fret lined up with the end of the body.

Hold or clamp the neck in the mortice and using a long straightedge along the centre of the fingerboard measure the height of the bottom of the straightedge above the bridge position. The finished measurement here should be 17mm, but at this point it is likely to be higher as the mortice is probably shallower than it might be. Also measure the over-stand of the neck at the body join. I aim for the bottom of the fingerboard to be 4-5mm above the bindings for the non-laminated style. It is worthwhile revisiting the original diagram drawn to calculate the neck angle and recalculating, if needed, the correct mortice depth.

Adjust the mortice depth with a back saw and chisels, or use the routing jig. This jig is a prototype and after fellow luthier Phill Kearney suggested pre-routing the mortice it hasn't been used. It cradles the instrument with various clamps and the plate on top holds the router at the correct angle.

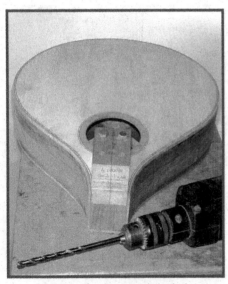

The setup for the second two holes

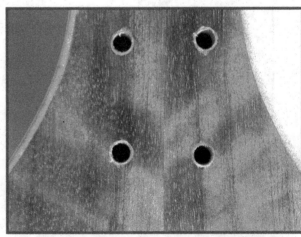

The neck bolt access holes in the back

The bar at the back of the plate holds it the appropriate distance from the soundboard at the bridge position and the front of the plate can be adjusted to set the correct depth of cut. I had several perspex templates made for various size necks, and a 1/2" ball bearing guide router bit indexes off the template to cut the mortice.

There are several obvious ways the jig can be made to work better and it could be adaptable for other kinds of instruments/

The danger with the jig is the end of the left side (looking from above) of the mortice being ripped out by the bit as it exits. The danger isn't too great if the mortice depth is only being increased by a mm or two, but the bit is really going the wrong way at this point.

Once the neck is seated at the correct angle, the bolt holes can be drilled in the same manner as described previously. Two 25mm/1" and two 32mm/1 1/4" will be needed to bolt the neck on.

If using the lamination on the upper soundboard this now needs to be carved away so it comes up to the bottom of the fingerboard and flows smoothly into the rest of the soundboard. If the soundboard was made without the lamination, and the fingerboard extends past the end of the neck to gain an extra couple of frets a small support can be made from the same material as the neck and shaped to fit.

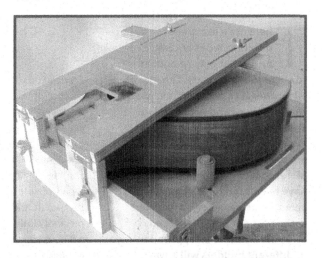

The routing jig with the body fitted

Routing the neck mortice

There are a number of different types of clear finish that may be applied to musical instruments. The idea of all finishes is to protect the timber from moisture and sweat and to enhance the appearance of the instrument in a way that does not adversely affect the ability of the plates to vibrate. Some finishes have been used for hundreds of years, some have been developed in the past decade. There is no one best finish for all applications as different builders will have differing expectations and access to methods of applying the finish. It is probably impractical to expect to have a spray booth set up in a high-rise apartment, but applying a french polish or water based acrylic finish is very conceivable. The body and neck are finished separately.

Choice of finish

French Polish
In its simplest form this is shellac flakes dissolved in alcohol. Commercially available French polish usually has one or more drying oils added to make the dried polish a little softer and flexible. Traditionally it is applied with a 'rubber', a pad of soft cloth that is saturated with the polish and then wrapped in another piece of cloth. This is applied in a circular rubbing motion which leaves a thin coat of polish with each application. It can also be sprayed, but it uses a lot more polish.
Plus - cheap, easy low-tech application, easily touched up or repaired
Minus - marked by moisture and skin contact, especially where a forearm comes in contact with the soundboard.

Varnish
Oil varnish is the finish most commonly used on high-quality violins. It is made by dissolving a hard organic resin in turpentine, which is a process full of alchemical mysteries and some danger. There are any number of recipes for varnish, many of which claim to be rediscoveries of the secret of the master seventeenth century violin makers. While serious violin builders cook up their own varnish, there are commercial varnishes available, mostly from German suppliers. There are also commercial oil varnishes available usually marketed for marine use. All need to be applied with a brush, then cut back and polished. Remember that violins do not come in contact with the player's body except for the neck, which is not varnished.
Plus - brush application
Minus - takes forever to dry (violin makers use cabinets with UV lights), stays quite soft and will get softer with body contact or it gets very hard and cracks.

Nitro-cellulose lacquer
Nitro-cellulose lacquer has been around since early last century and is essentially plant cellulose dissolved in nitric acid and thinned with rather nasty hydrocarbon solvents. It needs to be sprayed as the solvent thinners evaporate too quickly to allow brushing. (There are inhibitors available to slow down this evaporation, but I have never met anyone who uses them). It has been the industry standard finish for many upper end instruments since the 1920s. It needs to be applied in multiple coats as around 85% evaporates away.
Plus - clear, flexible finish that can be retouched or repaired.
Minus - needs spray equipment, thinners quite toxic and may annoy neighbours, multiple coats needed.

Water-based Acrylic
The toxicity of the solvents needed for solvent-based clear finishes has led to a growing demand for a water based finish that has the same 'look and feel' of nitro-cellulose. There are several brands available that are being used by instrument makers and doubtless more will be introduced in the future. Stewart McDonald and Luthiers Mercantile each sell at least one brand. They can be sprayed or brushed, though the water in them can corrode sprayguns (at least it did in my old one). A higher solids content means that less coats need to be applied and they do tend to look a little blue over Indian rosewood. The water-based clear finishes available in hardware stores tend to be softer when dry than those formulated for instrument building, but might well be used for a semi-gloss finish.
Plus - non-toxic, quick build, polishes well.
Minus - can corrode spray equipment.

Solvent based Acrylic

These are usually found in automotive shops and while they are applied in a similar way to nitro-cellulose lacquers, they do not set up as hard and can be quite easily marked or scratched. The thinners are quite toxic as well. Nevertheless this is a non coloured 'water-white' clear finish, but not as good as nitro-cellulose.

Plus - excellent clarity.

Minus - softness, toxic thinners.

Drying oils

Oil finishes are used sometimes in solid-body instruments and occasionally for acoustic ones, though I would not feel comfortable applying anything that soaked into a soundboard. For backs, sides and necks an oil finish is quite feasible combined with a french polished soundboard. When used on an opened grained timber the pore structure will be very obvious, but this might not be a bad thing.

Plus - ease of application (just wipe it on and polish it off), repairable.

Minus - doesn't have the smooth look of a lacquer.

Two-part Polyurethane/Polyester

Almost all of the guitars produced from the large factories in Asia are finished with a two-part polyurethane or polyester. This dries by a chemical reaction rather than evaporation of a solvent, so what gets sprayed on stays there. The mixed lacquer has a limited pot life, so if the spraygun isn't cleaned immediately after use you can throw it away because it won't be able to be used again. This kind of finish isn't really practical for occasional use, being better suited for continuous factory operations, but an automotive panel repair shop might be able to spray an instrument with a clear top coat if no other option was available.

Plus - very hard.

Minus - hard to repair and touch-up.

Recommendations

For all the advances in water based acrylics in recent years, nitro-cellulose lacquer is still used by many builders and does look good. If spraying nitro-cellulose is not an option, brushing a water based acrylic or French polishing will create an excellent finish.

Preparation

There are four stages to preparing the instrument for applying the final finish coats:
- gap filling
- grain filling
- sanding
- masking

The secret to a good finish is to have a smooth and flat surface over which the finish is applied. A slight gap around the bindings is barely noticeable at this point, but becomes a yawning chasm that sucks in a seemingly infinite amount of lacquer or polish when trying to sand it flat.

Gap filling

By this point the instrument will have been sanded to 120 grit. The soundboard, back and sides should be smooth, without ripples and with the corners of the bindings smoothly curving from the sides to the back and top plates. The neck shaft should be straight without lumps and flare smoothly to the head and heel. The idea of sanding with increasingly finer grades of sandpaper is just to remove the scratches left by the coarser grades. The basic shaping and smoothing will have been done by the 80 grit paper. The 120 grit should remove the deeper scratches from the 80 grit, but still needs a couple of finer grades as these sanding marks will still be visible under a finish.

Go over the body and neck with a stiff brush and/or compressed air (a spray gun without the fluid container works well) to get rid of all the dust. Check for any gaps around the bindings. They will need to be filled with a filler made from sanding dust and a binding agent. If for example the instrument has been made with a mahogany body and rosewood bindings any gaps should be filled with a paste made from rosewood dust and Titebond. If there are chips out of the mahogany from cutting the binding channels fill these with a filler made from mahogany dust and thinned lacquer. Mixing the dust with Titebond will darken the dust while mixing it with thinned lacquer will look darker when mixed, but will revert to the same colour as the dust when dry. This is useful when repairing any dents or gaps around the soundboard when mixed with dust sanded from the soundboard with 180 grit paper. The dried filler will shrink when dry, so a couple of applications may be necessary. The Titebond-based filler will need to be left overnight to dry, but the lacquer-based fillers will dry in a couple of hours.

Sand flat with 120 grit paper, being careful to sand any glue away that is left on the surface around the filled patches. This glue will be very noticeable under a finish.

Grain filling and sanding

An open pored timber like mahogany or rosewood will need to have the grain filled prior to applying the final finish. Oil-based paste grain fillers or water based fillers are available in a number of colours. The filler colour needs to be a shade or two darker than the wood to be filled, keeping in mind that the wood will darken with age and it looks better with a darker filler. Fillers can be darkened with wood stain if required.

An oil-based filler needs to be rubbed on and then removed with a coarse cloth rubbed across the grain before the 'wet look' has fully gone. It then need to dry for 48 hours to allow the mineral turpentine solvent to evaporate. Final sanding of the back, sides and neck can then be done with 180 grit, then 240 grit paper.

Water-based fillers can be applied with the fingers and sanded off when dry. Final sanding should then be done in the same way.

When sanding the neck extra care should be given to the areas where the end grain is exposed - the flare into the head and where the neck shaft again flares into the square section mortised into the body or the heel.

It is best to leave the soundboard until last for final sanding. A clear finish will show any imperfections in the sanding of a softwood. Care must be taken to hand sand along the grain, as any scratches even slightly across the grain will be obvious, or use an orbital sander. Whatever material that was used for the rosette will be harder than the softwood soundboard, and will have a tendency to end up as fine coloured dust embedded in, or at least discolouring, the area around the rosette.

Start with 120 grit, then 180, 280 grit for the soundboard. After the 280 grit spray the soundboard with water (using a laundry handsprayer) to raise the grain and to see any large scratches which may have been overlooked.

Masking and fitting handles

The fingerboard should be masked off with masking tape. The tape should cover the nut slot and the body end of the fretboard, which should have been sanded smooth in the same way as the rest of the neck. There is no real need to spray the face veneer of the head, though most builders do. Tightening the nuts that hold the machine heads on will indent any lacquer on the headstock face, and can even break the bond of the lacquer to the veneer. A rosewood or ebony veneer can be polished and buffed in the same way as the fingerboard, though if a lighter coloured veneer is used it would be worthwhile lacquering it.

The interior of the body should be vacuumed and/or blown clean of dust and shavings. If using a heel-less neck it is still worthwhile to cover the inside of the holes that extend through the back, as the air-pressure of a spray gun will stir up the inevitable bits that haven't been removed and send debris shooting out the holes to settle into the wet lacquer.

Handles need to be made so the body and neck can be held while spraying or polishing. Two narrow strips of 12mm (1/2" ply) a little narrower than the neck and around 300mm (1') long are cut and 7mm holes drilled to match the neck mounting holes. Two holes are sufficient. The neck is attached with a couple of appropriate-length bolts with the heads of the bolts wrapped in a strip of masking tape to keep them clean. If using a neck with a heel, this handle should be a couple of millimetre narrower than the body mortice with the holes drilled to match.

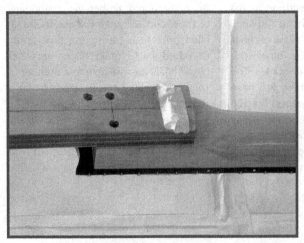

Handle for a heel-less neck

Handle for a body useing a heeled neck

The handle for the body is fixed with two bolts with wing nuts which can be fitted either inside or outside. Again cover either the bolt head or the wing nut with masking tape. A sponge rubber block the depth of the body is inserted into the soundhole and covered with a disc of card 10mm greater diameter than the soundhole.

Give body and neck a final blow with compressed air and/or a wipe down with a tackrag to remove any remaining dust.

Spraying lacquer

Spraying nitro-cellulose or acrylic lacquer is inherently a dangerous procedure. The fumes are both highly flammable and toxic and it should be done in a properly constructed spray-booth fitted with the correct filters and flame/spark proof extractor fans and lighting. It is often illegal not to have this equipment for sound environmental reasons. Nevertheless, with care spraying can be done outside in the open air preferably on a sunny day with a bit of a breeze, and preferably when the neighbours are out. A good-quality mask is necessary, fitted with the proper filters.

Remarkably cheap compressor/spraygun packages are available, usually made in China or Taiwan and while probably not suitable for heavy duty industrial use are fine for spraying musical instruments. A gun with a 1.5-2mm nozzle is required. Recent years have seen the introduction of high-volume/low-pressure (HVLP) spraying equipment, which uses a lot less lacquer, but the setup cost are much higher.

Most manufacturers of nitro-cellulose lacquers make a product formulated for musical instruments and around a litre/quart and the same amount of thinners will be necessary for an instrument. Sanding sealer, which is lacquer with a quantity of talc added, is useful for a base coat and to build a totally flat surface for the gloss top coats, but too much of it sitting in the grain of the wood can become opaque and it is not totally necessary.

Sealer and lacquer will need to be thinned with up to 50% thinners, but this will depend on the lacquer itself, the gun used and the pressure from the compressor. It needs to hit the wood from 6-8" away while still 'wet', but not so wet that it runs, but not so thick that it dries before it reaches the sprayed surface. Spraying pressure will usually be around 30psi, but experiment with pressure, thinners and the controls on the gun before starting on the instrument.

I was taught originally to spray three double coats of sealer, leave to dry overnight and then sand flat with 280 or 360 grit paper. Three double coats of gloss lacquer are then sprayed each day with a day or two drying time, sanding between until a flat surface is attained. This can entail four or five days of spraying. The instrument is then left for a week or more for final drying and then the lacquer is cut back with 600 and 1200 wet and dry paper then buffed to a high gloss.

A technique developed by Michael Pemberthy of Gilet Guitars works just as well with less coats and less sanding - which can only be a good thing! Michael sprays three double coats on successive days without cutting back, straight onto the grain filled timber. It is left for three days before a vigorous cutting back with 180 grit (though I use 280 on the soundboard). Another three double coats are sprayed and left for a week before final cutting back and polishing.

Michael has been doing this for many years and is very skilled at getting the maximum amount of lacquer on without any runs, and less skilled sprayers may need an extra day's worth of spraying. The critical factor is the time left before sanding, as this allows the solvents trapped in the lacquer to fully evaporate and any shrinkage to occur. Sanding back too early means obvious pores in the wood and highlights any little glue join gaps.

The final polishing to a high gloss is a matter of sanding away to smaller and smaller scratches in the lacquer. Although I don't go past a 1200 grit wet and dry paper, there are much finer papers available, up to 5000 grit. The final shine can be obtained with Brasso or a paste buffing compound (from an automotive shop, but one without silicones) and a soft cloth, buffing wheel or pad. Every builder will have their own way of spraying and polishing and techniques will differ according to the brand and formulation of the lacquer used.

Water-based acrylics

I never had a great deal of success spraying water-based finishes, though I am perfectly willing to admit that it was more me than the finish itself. It would clog up the gun or dry before it got to the surface and never seemed to polish up just right, though I wasn't using a buffing wheel which I suspect is one of the secrets.

An article by Michael Turko in *American Lutherie* No 72 provides a useful technique for applying KTM-4 acrylic with a brush that is quick and practical. With his permission, the following is the basics of his method though the full article should be read to get all the little tricks that he has worked out. I don't know how this will work with other brands of water-based acrylics, but it would seem worth a try. It also uses a lot less finish than spraying.

The surface is first sealed with one or more coats of shellac. This adds a base colour or tint and seals the wood from absorbing any of the moisture in the lacquer itself. The KTM is then applied with a 2" foam brush, loading the brush with a lot of the finish and moving the brush slowly in slightly overlapping strokes. A second coat is applied with a brush, as well as using a credit card to pack it into the pores or any gaps, and when dry a third coat is applied with the foam brush.

After drying overnight, sand with 220 grit paper, just to take the ridges off. Apply another three coats with the foam brush, let dry overnight and sand again. Fill any low spots with little blobs of the KTM and sand again after drying. The credit card, fingers or the foam brush can be used to flatten the lacquer and push it into any little dips or gaps. After one more coat with the foam brush the entire surface should be able to be sanded completely flat. Michael then uses a french polishing technique of a golf ball size wad of old t-shirt to wipe on a thin top coat, filling in the 220 grit scratches. Final sanding is done is a 30 micron plastic backed sanding disk from 3M (I don't know what 30 microns translates into as a grit size, but I am sure it is very fine). The instrument is then polished on a buffing wheel.

Michael also points out that any runs or drips should be cut away with a sharp blade, rather than trying to sand them away and warns to keep any trace of oil away from the KTM. The manufacturers of KTM also supply a 'crosslinker' which is added in a small proportion to the final coats to make it harder and able to take a higher gloss.

This approach is a very cost effective way to finish an instrument, and Michael says it can be done entirely in a weekend.

The function of the bridge is to transfer the energy of the plucked strings to the soundboard. It is usual to use hard and dense timbers such as ebony or rosewood which will not absorb the strings' vibrations, but pass them through to the soundboard. On an arch-top instrument the bridge must be closely fitted to the curvature of the soundboard and atailpiece must be made to hold the strings at the end of the body.

String length compensation

When fretting a string - pushing it down to contact the fret - it gets stretched and the pitch will be raised. How much the pitch gets raised is dependent on the gauge of the string (or in the case of wound strings, the gauge of the core wire) with the pitch of thicker strings being raised more than thinner ones. This why guitar builders add 3mm or so to the theoretical scale for the top e string when fixing the bridge position and the saddle slot is angled so the contact point for the bottom E string is up to 6-8mm longer than the scale length.

This is called compensation and works as well as possible to help the instruments play in tune. Some guitars builders use a wider saddle than the standard 3/32" and set the compensation for each string individually by comparing the octave harmonic at the 12th fret with the fretted note and moving the saddle contact point until they match.

The tuning and stringing of four-course octave mandolin tuned instruments means staggered saddle contact points similar to a Gibson wooden mandolin bridge, so the saddle slot needs to be parallel to the front of the bridge and 5mm wide to cope with the necessary compensation. Adding a fifth course, higher or lower, complicates matters by requiring at least the 5mm of saddle width compensation available, if not a little more. 6mm wide bone is available, but it is making the bridge of an archtop instrument rather wide if using a removable saddle. More on that later in the chapter.

Compensation is a compromise, but tuning any fretted instrument is a compromise anyway, so we have to live with it.

The pin bridge

The classical guitar developers of the various styles of lattice bracing styles have found that a smaller and narrower bridge works better. The bridge also acts as a cross grain brace, and while this design doesn't have the stiffening lattice underneath the bridge, the cross grain bridge plate and relatively narrow bridge perform the same function.

The bridge is made from ebony or rosewood that has been thicknessed to 11mm with the front edge planed or sanded straight and vertical. Mark the centre point and the length of the saddle. Saddle length will depend on the number of courses and any installation of an under-saddle pickup. The spacing between of the outside strings at the saddle should be the same as the width of the fingerboard at the 12th fret. Allow 6-8mm on either side of the outside strings, unless an under-saddle guitar pickup is going to be used which is designed for a 72mm length guitar saddle slot.

If using a guitar pickup make sure it is one with a full width sensing element, not one with six discrete piezo crystals. Strips of masking tape are useful as a visual indicator at each end of the slot when routing.

Attach the blank to the bridge slotting jig using 2 x 3/16" bolts and wingnuts through what will be waste areas of the bridge blank (and that are well out of the way of the router bit). Fit the router with a 5mm or 3/16" straight bit and a fence set so the front edge of the slot will be 4mm from the front of the blank. Taking shallow cuts of 2-3mm, rout the slot leaving 3mm of wood under the bottom of the slot.

This can also be done with a milling machine or a drill press fitted with an X/Y sliding vice.

Remove the bridge blank from the slotting jig and mark the string positions, working in from the outside strings. The string spacings are not regular, the top strings being at 2.5mm centres, increasing to 4mm apart for the bottom strings. The spacing between courses increases from 9mm between the first and second courses to 10.5mm between the third and fourth courses (or fourth and fifth). The drawings have all the measurements.

The holes for the front pins are drilled 8mm from the back of the saddle slot with the second row 9mm behind that. Mark the position with a brad awl and drill the holes with a 5/32" drill.

Mark the finished bridge outline on the blank and cut it out on the bandsaw. Finish shaping with a disk sander (to square off the ends) and a sanding drum or chisels to shape the back of the bridge. Use the disk sander to reduce the height of the bridge to 9mm at the treble end of the saddle slot rising to 10.5mm at the bass end and curved to follow the radius of the fingerboard.

This will ensure that there will be an even height of the saddle above the top of the bridge, and the break angle of the strings will be consistent, which is important if there is a pickup installed. Use chisels and sandpaper to thin the wings of the bridge to 3mm, scooping down from the ends of the saddle slot to the 3mm thickness. Thin out the centre section of the bridge using the disk sander behind the saddle slot so the back edge is 3-4mm high.

Countersink the holes drilled for the bridge pins to the size of the heads of the bridge pins. It will look a little neater if the bridge can be supported so the sloping rear section is horizontal, but it is not strictly necessary. Sand with 120, 180 and 240 grit sandpaper, then 400 and 600 grit wet & dry and then buff with a polish or on a buffing wheel.

Using the router saddle slot jig

Cutting the saddle slot with an X/Y sliding vice on a drill press

Four-course pin bridge

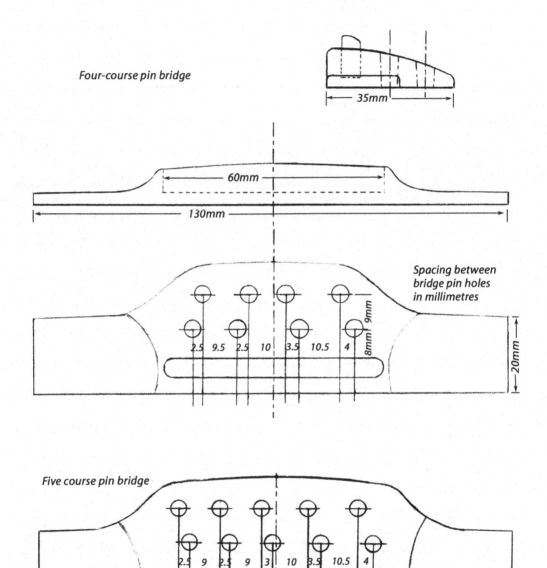

35mm

60mm

130mm

Spacing between
bridge pin holes
in millimetres

2.5 9.5 2.5 10 3.5 10.5 4   8mm 9mm

20mm

Five course pin bridge

2.5 9 2.5 9 3 10 3.5 10.5 4

70mm

Positioning and gluing the bridge

Bolt the neck to the body, checking that the neck is centred on the body centreline. Using a long straightedge ruler or an Ibex fret ruler, establish an approximate bridge position and cover the area of the bridge with masking tape, overlapping the bridge area by 20mm on all sides. Draw a centreline on the tape and then mark the scale length plus 3mm across that line. Mark another line 4mm forward of the first, and this will be the front of the bridge with the top string contact point at the front of the saddle. Draw a line perpendicular to the centreline at this position that is the same length as the bridge and centre the front of the bridge on this line, holding it in position with a couple of extra strips of masking tape.

Check the lateral positioning of the bridge by holding the straightedge so it follows the line of the outermost strings from the nut to the saddle. The nut slot for the outside top string will be centred 2mm in from the fingerboard edge at the nut and the outside bass string will be centred 3.5mm from the edge.

The straightedge should follow a line just about parallel to the edge of the fingerboard when checked on both sides. If not, recheck the alignment of the neck. Even a very small misalignment of the neck will cause the bridge position to be thrown out and the strings have to be running along the neck correctly.

Now recheck all the measurements. The bridge has to be in the right position, and if it is not, it is a very tedious job to get it right. Check that the front of the bridge slot is the scale length (ie twice the nut to 12th fret distance) plus 3mm from the nut. Check that the front of the bridge is the same distance from each end of the last fret - ie that the front of the bridge is parallel with the frets. Hold the bridge in position with two long clamps on the wings and drill through the two outside bridge pin holes. Use two 18mm or 3/4" countersunk head 5/32" bolts and wingnuts to hold the bridge in position and scribe around the outside of the bridge with a new Exacto knife blade, angling the blade in slightly under the bridge if possible.

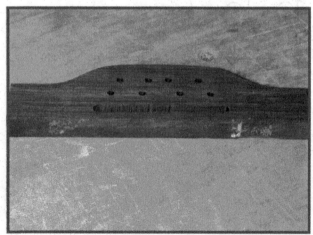

The bridge cut to shape with the saddle slot routed and the bridge pin holes drilled

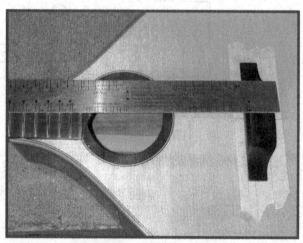

Establishing the bridge position

The objective is to cut through the masking tape and the lacquer without cutting into the soundboard itself. Cut away from the corners, not towards them, to avoid cutting past the bridge itself.

Remove the bridge and peel away the masking tape where the bridge was. With a very sharp 10-12mm chisel cut away the lacquer, being careful of the grain runout of the soundboard and chipping near the edges.

When finished, peel away the rest of the masking tape and the bridge can be glued on. If using a rosewood bridge, wipe down the bottom surface with acetone to remove the oils. Cover the bottom of the bridge with a thin coat of Titebond, and position it with the two bolts. Tighten the wingnuts from inside the body and clean up any glue squeezeout with a damp cloth and/or a plastic drinking straw cut at an angle (the big fat ones from McDonalds are really good).

Fit three long clamps through the soundhole (either long wooden cam clamps or dedicated bridge clamps) and clamp the two wings, then the centre of the bridge. Use softwood or cork cauls to avoid marking the bridge. Clean up the squeezeout, which can be a bit tricky around the clamps, but get as much of it off as possible.

Leave overnight to dry, remove the clamps and bolts and clean up any remaining dried glue with a cloth and warm water. Drill out the remaining bridge pin holes and ream them out to the correct size with a bridge pin reamer. If you haven't got one, a 3/16" drill will do, but a tapered hole works better.

The archtop bridge and pickups

There are differing opinions as to the best size, mass and material to build an archtop bridge. The standard for the past 80 years has been the Gibson-style two-part, two footed, thumb-wheel adjustable bridge with the necessary compensation carved in the top section. Apart from not believing that it is optimal for the vibrations of the strings to be transmitted to the soundboard through two metal posts, there is no simple way of fitting an under-saddle pickup (well, there is no removable saddle for a start!) which is the simplest, if perhaps not the most accurate, way of amplifying an instrument for stage use.

Robert Bennedetto suggests in *Making an Archtop Guitar* that a light bridge made from maple following the principles of violin bridges will be superior, but acknowledges that many players want the adjustability of the traditional bridge.

The lacquer cut away from under the bridge position

The bridge glued and clamped with the locating bolts

In his 1998 lecture at the Guild of American Luthiers conference and in an article in *American Lutherie* on the work of James D'Aquisto, John Monteleone expresses his preference for a relatively wide based bridge that is in contact with the soundboard across it's whole surface, suggesting that the bridge acts as another soundboard brace.

He also sees the acoustic limitations of the metal post/thumb-wheel construction and sees potential in further development of D'Aquisto's wedge adjustable bridge. In a similar way there is the Brekke mandolin bridge used by Weber Mandolins which uses set screws to push in wedges horizontally which can raise and lower the saddle.

Acoustically, these developments suggest that there are improvements to be made in the traditional Gibson-style bridges, but don't solve the problem of fitting any kind of guitar-type undersaddle pickups. The alternative is a soundboard transducer, which is attached to the inside of the soundboard, or an internally mounted microphone. The positioning of the transducer or microphone is critical in both cases and will require an amount of trial and error to get the optimal sound. The soundboard transducer is more subject to picking up general body noise, which can be annoying.

Fishman make archtop mandolin and guitar bridges with piezo elements installed in the upper sections, though the mandolin string spacing is narrower than my suggested bouzouki spacing. It may be possible to re-compensate the guitar model for a cittern, but it would depend on where in the top section of the bridge the piezo is fitted.

While happy to admit that under-saddle piezo pickups might not necessarily give the best and most accurate reproduction of an instrument's acoustic sound, their advantages for on-stage use in being able to simply 'plug in and play' outweigh their drawbacks. A good-quality pickup, especially when combined with an internally mounted microphone, will work quite acceptably in most live circumstances. There are always new pickup designs coming onto the market, especially using thin film piezo which can be fitted between the bottom of the bridge and the soundboard. Who can predict what will be available in a few years?

This bridge is probably too heavy for optimal acoustic response, but it does allow fitting an under-saddle pickup under a removable saddle, the height of which may be varied for action adjustment, and the two-part construction will allow further modification to the height.

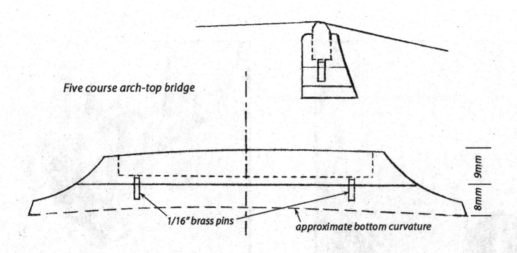

Five course arch-top bridge

1/16" brass pins *approximate bottom curvature*

8mm | 9mm

Making the bridge

This bridge contacts the soundboard across it's entire width and uses a separate saddle which allows the fitting of an under-saddle pickup if required. It is made in two pieces which locate together with 1/16" brass pins which means if there ever has to be some radical altering of the bridge height a shim could be inserted between the two parts or one part lowered in height. It can be made from one standard bridge blank in either rosewood or ebony.

The bridge blank should be thicknessed as thick as is practical (depending on the the original thickness of the blank, of course). This might simply be a matter of removing any saw marks and making sure the top and bottom surfaces are parallel as well as sanding or planing one edge straight and at right angles to the top and bottom. The saddle slot in the top half can be routed in the same way as described in the section on pin bridges, except rout the slot 3mm from the front edge.

Slice off the front 15mm of the bridge and square up the front of the remaining section. Slice off another 15mm section, which will be the bottom piece of the bridge. Clean up the sawn face and mark the 'up' side. This will keep the grain in both sections the same. The bottom of the second section will be fitted to the curve of the soundboard. Trim both to a little over 120mm in length, keeping the saddle slot in the middle of the top piece .

Hold the two blocks together with a couple of spring clamps, lining up the front faces and. Drill 2 x 1/16" holes through the bottom of the saddle slot right through the bottom section. Short brass pins will be fitted later which will keep the two sections in alignment.

Place a strip of 3/4" masking tape on the soundboard at the bridge position and mark with pencil the front of the bridge and its finished 120mm width. Hold the bridge bottom section in place and trace the soundboard curve with a pencil, making sure the curve is even across the width, so the top surface is horizontal. Cut most of the waste away on the bandsaw or chisel it off.

The curved bottom surface must match that of the soundboard exactly and this can be done in several ways. The reason for the strip of masking tape is that it can be rubbed with chalk, the bridge rubbed in it and the chalk carved or scraped away. This can be repeated until the chalk marks the whole bottom surface. There is likely to be a slight longitudinal as well as transverse curve in the soundboard and this has to be kept in mind. A small curved scraper is good for the final touches.

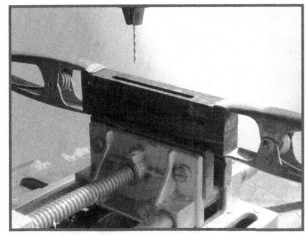

Drilling holes for the locating pins

Marking the soundboard curve

Alternatively the masking tape need not be used and a piece of 120 grit paper can be taped to the soundboard and the bridge fitted by rubbing back and forth, preferably with a jig to hold it vertical . The scraper can be used to scrape away the sanded bits and then sand again until the entire bottom surface has sanding marks. The danger is that bits of the sandpaper grit get dislodged, mixed up with the wood dust and can annoyingly scratch the just-polished soundboard. Best to do it this way before the final polishing!

Once the bottom section is fitted to the soundboard, the 17mm overall height of the bridge needs to be established. Hold the two bridge section together and measure the height from the centre of the curved bottom to the top. Mark 17mm and check that the depth of what would be the resulting saddle slot is still at least 6mm. If the saddle slot is going to end up too shallow the top face of the bottom section needs to be reduced.

Fit two short 1/16" brass pins into the holes in the bottom section so they project 2mm above the top surface. A drop of super glue might help hold them in place. The 2mm height means they will not project into the bottom of the saddle slot, which would be important if a pickup is to be installed. Fit the two bridge sections together.

Shape the top of the bridge to the curvature of the fretboard , making the treble side a millimetre lower. This will ensure an even projection of the saddle above the bridge top. Cut away the wings of the bridge from 5mm either end of the slot to the ends of the bridge 3mm high. This can be done on the bandsaw and finished with a small drum sander or chisels and sandpaper.

The front surface should be sanded smooth and the back of the bridge tapered from 12-13mm at the bottom to 10mm at the top. This can be done on a larger 3" drum sander in the drill press, which gives a pleasant concave curve to it, or it can simply be sanded flat. The idea is to remove as much mass as possible while still retaining enough strength in the top section to hold the saddle without splitting along the saddle slot. There should be at least 2mm in front and behind the slot.

The entire bridge should be sanded to 600 grit and then buffed on a buffing wheel.

If an under-saddle pickup is fitted this is the time to do it, as the thickness of the pickup itself will need to be taken into account when setting the saddle height. For an archtop instrument this adds the complication of what to do with the pickup lead.

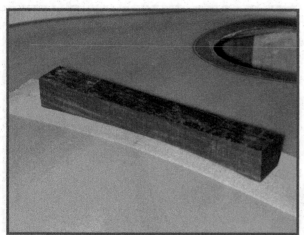

Using chalk covered & masking tape to find the high points on the bottom of the bridge

Shaping the ends of the bridge

For a pickup such as a Fishman Matrix with a lead at 90° to the pickup the lead can come out the back of the bridge through a curved slot and then taken down through a small hole drilled through the soundboard under the tailpiece.

For coaxial pickups like the Headway or Highlander the only way I have worked out is to drill the required shallow angled hole though the bridge and soundboard. This requires the bridge to be fixed to the soundboard, which is not normally done with arch-top bridges as there is an expectation that the the soundboard will change shape slightly in the first couple of years and the bridge may need to be refitted for optimal contact.

The alternative is for the bridge to move, as it will almost certainly, and eventually wear through the pickup lead or, in the case of the Headway or Highlander, the coaxial pickup itself. All that is necessary is for the bridge to be held in place; a small drop of superglue on each end will do that, and be removable if that is needed.

The bridge has to be placed with the same care as with a pin-bridge, so the calculated compensated top string saddle contact position is just inside the bridge slot. Remember, measure everything at least twice, if not three times, before applying the super glue. Strips of masking tape around the perlmeter of the bridge will assist in keeping it in the right place.

The Tailpiece

The important thing about a bouzouki/ cittern tailpiece is that it should take ball-end strings, if for no other reason that it is hard to find the correct gauges in loop-end strings. While the ball ends can be crushed and removed, it is all too easy to break the loop while doing so, and making a tailpiece to take ball end strings is not hard.

The simplest approach is to fabricate one from sheet brass with slots to accept the ball ends. Many fine makers like Stefan Sobell have used these for years. The one disadvantage of these is that the length of string between the bridge and tailpiece is prone to sympathetic resonance, more likely than not at pitches that do not sit comfortably with the tuning of the instrument. Many players resort to strips of leather woven between the strings to damp them.

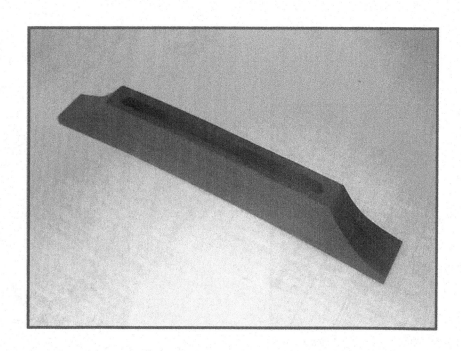

The alternative is a tailpiece similar to those used on archtop guitars. Most contemporary archtop builders have gone away from the metal trapeze tailpiece, preferring to make them from ebony with some form of metal hinge that screws into the tailblock or in the Bennadetto style using a nylon cello tailpiece fastener. A look through Ken Vose's *Blue Guitar* (Chronicle Books, 1998) will show a variety of approaches, both traditional and modern.

This design was inspired by the tailpieces used on viols where the tailpiece pivots on a square wooden post. The string tension of a bouzouki being rather heavier than a viol, a length of 1/4" x 1/4" brass rod was used for the support. The tailpiece has a strip of brass sheet inset into it's bottom surface with a hole drilled to take the rod which has a notch machined for the sheet to pivot on. This single point bearing means the tailpiece is free to find it's own level in two dimensions.

There are a variety of ways to hold the string ball-ends. The keyhole slots such as are used on violin tailpieces and the Bennadetto style tailpieces are tricky to machine without a mill or at least an X-Y sliding vice on a drill press. They do tend to force the tailpiece down towards the soundboard without a support under the hinge end to keep it up. (see Robert Bennadetto's *Making an Archtop Guitar)* The advantage of these tailpieces is that they can be made quite thin and light, but it can be quite hard to just change one string.

The other approach is a ramped slot of some kind machined across the tailpiece blank and longitudinal holes drilled from the bridge end to meet the slot. I built a jig that would hold a block of ebony with a ramp to slide a router down, but it was a messy process that covered the workshop in ebony dust and shavings and the resultant shape of the bridge was never entirely satisfactory.

The most recent method uses a pocket hole jig, usually used by furniture makers to drill angled slots for screws to hold frames together. They drill a 3/8" hole at a 15° angle which is big enough to take two ball-ends side by side, and the rest of the tailpiece can be sculpted around the four or five holes necessary. The angled holes should end 10mm or 3/8" from the bridge end of tailpiece which gives enough mass of timber to take the tension. Most of the larger mail-order or on-line woodworking tool shops have one or more pocket-hole setups available.

The end of the tailpiece should be 60-65mm from the bridge. Any less than 55mm seems to tighten up and constrict the sound. It is worth considering that violin makers work to a strict after-bridge length of 55mm which means that the length of string should sound in an exact harmonic of the playing length.

The tailpiece blank with the string slots drilled with a pocket-hole jig

Drilling the string holes

There is some useful experimental work to be done to find an ideal proportional bridge to tailpiece length for bouzoukis/citterns and probably arch-top guitars as well.

A number of archtop guitar makers angle the end of the tailpiece so the after-bridge length is longer on the bass side. John Monteleone prefers to have the treble strings longer as he finds the longer length gives more flexibility in the playing length of the strings which is good for bending the strings. This is probably not so important for bouzouki or cittern players.

Thickness the tailpiece blank to 12mm and of even width. This thickness will have the holes ending 2mm from the bottom when drilled to finish 10mm from the end. Sand the bridge end square and mark the centre lines of the necessary number of angled holes (in this case - 5). Mount the tailpiece block in the jig and drill the holes, using the stop collar to establish the depth.

The tailpiece should start 60mm from the back of the bridge and extend 10mm past the end of the instrument to allow room for the support post. Calculate the length of the tailpiece and trim to length. A slot needs to be machined along the centre of the bottom surface of the blank to accept a 50mm strip of 2mm brass sheet. The exact width is not important, but 18-20mm is sufficient. I use a dovetail bit in the router table which undercuts the edges and helps hold the strip in place but this is not essential. Drill a 3mm deep, 10mm hole centred 8mm from the end to accept the support post and an 8mm hole in the brass strip positioned so the front edge of the 8mm hole is in line with the front of the 10mm hole. Three short (1/4") screws should be fitted through the strip to fix it to the blank.

The brass support post should be cut to length so it will start just above the strap button or pickup output socket which will be centred on the butt strip. It needs to extend 5mm above the bindings. File a 1mm deep x 2mm wide notch on one side starting 2mm from the top of the post. The back edge of the hole in the brass strip will fit into this notch.

Round the edges of the post from the bottom of the notch up so it will fit through the 8mm hole in the strip. Check that the tailpiece is held just by the brass strip and that the post is not bearing on the couple of millimetres of wood behind the 10mm hole. The string tension will crack the wood and it will need superglue and dust to fix it later.

Drilling a 10mm hole for the support post

The finished tailpiece

Two holes 10 and 30mm from the bottom should be drilled in the support post for mounting screws and the tailpiece carved to whatever shape you want, keeping in mind the various holes and screws. It should be around 10mm thick in the middle, thinning out towards the edges. Sand to 600 grit and buff.

Drill two holes in the butt strip of the body to match the holes drilled in the brass post, and positioned so that the post protrudes 5mm above the binding. Attach the post with the two screws.

The underneath of the tailpiece showing the brass bearing plate

The tailpiece mounting post

This is the final stage of the construction, and the point at which the wooden box can start making music. The frets have to be levelled and re-profiled, the machine heads fitted, a nut fitted and shaped and a saddle similarly shaped and adjusted for height and intonation.

The frets

It is easier to level the frets on a heel-less neck while separated from the body, but the heeled neck is best done after the neck is bolted on as the fingerboard will then be supported along its entire length.

Tighten the trussrod nut so it just bears against the brass block, without putting any backwards force on the neck. The neck should be as straight as possible for this procedure. The tops of the frets have to ground down so the tops of the frets are all at the same level along the neck. The transverse curvature of the fingerboard means that the top surface of the frets is close to a section of a long shallow cone, so a straight edge will contact along the length of the fingerboard, but not at an angle across the fingerboard.

If the fingerboard itself was carefully levelled and the frets inserted evenly, little should be needed to be taken off the top of the frets to obtain a flat bevel across the entire width of each fret.

This can be done with a carborundum or silicon carbide stone, a file at least 200mm (8") long or one of the speciality tools sold by lutherie suppliers. Whatever tool is used should be used going along the length of the fingerboard. A tool that can be gripped firmly is preferable. A silicon carbide sharpening stone is good as it has weight, can be held and many are double sided so the fine side can be used for finishing off any slight irregularities in the fret height

Jim Williams suggests using a blue or green marker pen to highlight the top of each fret before starting. In any case, with an oblique light source, the shiny newly cut bevel on the top of the frets can usually be seen quite clearly.

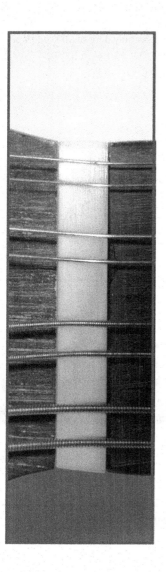

Leveling the frets with a sharpening stone

If there are one or more frets from which it seems that there is a lot being removed, and the frets either side are not being touched, or barely marked, it can be useful to tap that fret down a little with the fretting hammer, as it is likely it is not sitting firmly on the fingerboard.

It is likely that there was some buildup of finish along the edge of the fingerboard, along the edge of the masking tape on the fingerboard itself. The angled bevel on the ends of the frets should be cleaned up with a file or the stone and a slight bevel - .5mm or 1/64" - can be ground along the edge of the fingerboard and the bottom of the frets. This helps to keep any sharp edges on the bottom of the frets away from the pads of the playing fingers.

Any remaining edges of lacquer, or any that has seeped under the masking tape can be scraped away with an Exacto knife or a single edged razor blade

The frets now need to be re-crowned with a fret file which has a concave groove the same width as the frets. The flat bevel should be filed away until there is just the suggestion of the flat in the middle of the fret. The angle at the ends of the frets needs to be gently rounded off with the file held up at an angle while being careful not to put grooves into the fingerboard itself. There are speciality tools for this, and while useful, are not essential.

The entire fingerboard should now be sanded with 600 grit wet & dry paper to remove all the file marks. The fingerboard surface should also be sanded at the same time, paying attention to where the frets meet the fingerboard and cleaning out any goop that has accumulated there. Sanding should be done both across and along the frets.

Follow the 600 grit with 1200 grit wet & dry in the same way and polish with Brasso or other metal polish using a paper towel or soft cloth. This can leave a white residue in the pores of fingerboard material like rosewood, but can be removed with alcohol.

Avoid using steel wool as the little fragments of it get caught up in unwanted places, and even 0000 grade steel wool is only the equivalent of 600 grit paper.

Re-crowning the frets with a fret file

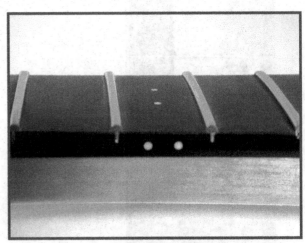

The finished polished frets

Fitting the machine heads

The holes drilled in the head might well need cleaning out from lacquer and grain filler. A violin peg reamer is the best tool for this or a round file will do if care is taken not to chip the lacquer on the edge of the holes.

If four-on-a-plate mandolin tuners are used the bushings will have to press fitted into the holes. The bushing should be able to be 'finger-pushed' in so they are 1mm proud of the head surface. They can be pushed in the rest of the way with the head held in a vice, with a smooth softwood caul on the lacquered back of the head to avoid any marks. The plates themselves can be fitted and 1/16" holes drilled for the retaining screws.

Individual heads can be fitted with the shafts for the tuning buttons at right angles to the edge of the head.

The trussrod cover

If the trussrod is adjustable from the head end, the slot cut through the head overlay should be covered with a small piece of wood, preferably the same as the head overlay, though a contrasting piece would work fine as well. This can be a bullet shape, with the sides bevelled in and fixed with one or two small countersunk screws.

Lining up the edges of the machine heads with a short ruler

Tightening the top locking nuts

The truss-rod nut cover

The nut

The nut at the end of the fingerboard serves both to establish the string separation and height. It is usually made from bone or man-made materials of similar density such as Corian (a resin impregnated with marble dust), Micarta (used by Martin), Tusq (a synthetic ivory) or carbon graphite composites. Avoid soft moulded plastics such as are found on cheap guitars. Ordinary bone works just fine and is the cheapest, but there is a certain attraction about using something exotic like fossilised mammoth ivory.

Sand the nut to thickness so it sits firmly in the 5mm gap left between the fingerboard and the head overlay. Reduce the width so it follows the curve of the neck into the flair of the head. The widest point should be about halfway up the thickness of the fingerboard with a slight curve inwards above the top of the fingerboard.

The front of the nut needs to be slightly more than a string thickness higher than the frets - .015" (.32mm) on the treble side and .045" (1.2mm) on the bass side.

A stub of pencil will give an approximate mark on the nut when run across the fingerboard and the height should be checked with a short straight edge. File or sand down to the pencil mark, angling the top back at the same angle as the head.

The outside treble string sits 2mm in from the edge of the fingerboard, with its pair 2mm further in. The outside bass string is 3.5mm in from the edge of the fingerboard with its pair 3.5mm further in. These measurements are to the centre of the string groove. The spacing between the courses increases as the strings get heavier, to keep the distance between the courses approximately even. The diagram on page *** gives the string and course spacings for both four- and five-course instrument .

At this point mark the slot positions and file a shallow groove, just enough to locate the strings. Don't glue it in at this time, but a very small drop of super glue on the front face of the nut where it touches the end of the fingerboard will hold it in place once the grooves are finalised.

The nut should be sanded to at least 180 grit, though many makers go much finer and polish the bone. The only problem with doing that is that it makes it slippery and harder to file the slots later.

The saddle

Like the nut, the saddle has the dual role of establishing the string height and spacing but at the bridge end. A pin bridge will space the strings according to the placement of the pin holes, but grooves in the saddle can help in keeping them in the right place. On an arch-top instrument grooves almost the depth of the string are needed to set the string spacing and not have them move while the instrument is being played heavily.

All this is complicated by the necessity of adding 3-6mm of string length to the theoretical scale to compensate for the strings being stretched a little sharp as they are pressed to the fingerboard.

Marking the nut height

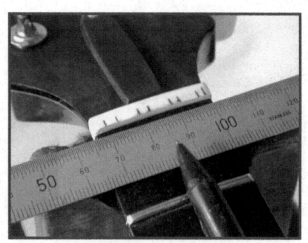

Laying out the nut slots

Because of the tuning of a bouzouki/
cittern and the strings used, the saddle
compensation is similar to that used on
mandolins. This is why the saddle slot was
routed parallel to the front of the bridge
and 5mm wide. Large bone saddles are
available from suppliers or man-made
materials can be used.

I often use Corian, cut from a block
obtained from a kitchen manufacturer,
especially for instruments with pickups,
as it seems to help iron out any string-to-
string balance problems.

The saddle needs to be sanded to
thickness and length so it is a smooth
press fit in the saddle slot. It is important
that it can't flop around backwards and
forwards.

The centre of the top surface of the bridge
(whether fixed or floating) should be in
the same plane as the centreline of the
fingerboard, with the treble side of the
bridge slightly higher and the bass side
slightly lower. This will ensure an even
saddle height above the bridge and
helps a lot with balancing the strings
when an undersaddle pickup is fitted by
maintaining an even break angle of the
strings across the saddle.

If an undersaddle pickup is to be fitted
insert it into the saddle slot at this point to
save having to lower the saddle later.

Initially shape the saddle so it protrudes
4mm above the bridge and file grooves
for the strings spaced as per the diagram.

The diagrams opposite give a good
indication of where the saddle contact
points need to be on different saddles.
The saddle can be shaped according to
the diagrams, or this can wait until after
stringing up and an electronic tuner used
as describing in the next section.

Marking the saddle slots

Filing the saddle string slots.
The compensation ramps have been filed

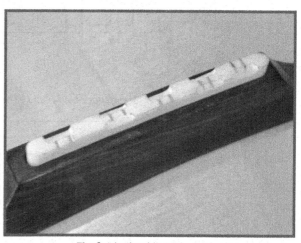

The finished saddle in the bridge

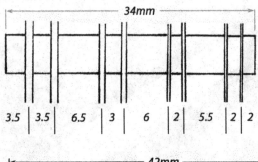

34mm

| 3.5 | 3.5 | 6.5 | 3 | 6 | 2 | 5.5 | 2 | 2 |

String spacing are suggested and can be varied to suit individual requirements. The thicker, wound strings should be a little further apart than the plain strings. It means the courses are not centred on the fingerboard, but it is preferred.

Note: string spacings are centre to centre of the slots.

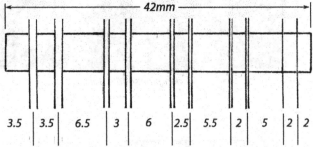

42mm

| 3.5 | 3.5 | 6.5 | 3 | 6 | 2.5 | 5.5 | 2 | 5 | 2 | 2 |

String spacing for a four and five course nut

String spacing and saddle conact points for a four course instrument

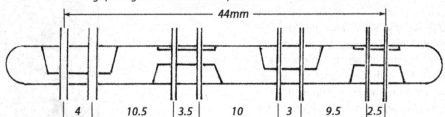

44mm

| 4 | 10.5 | 3.5 | 10 | 3 | 9.5 | 2.5 |

String spacing and saddle contact points for a five-course instrument using a plain third course

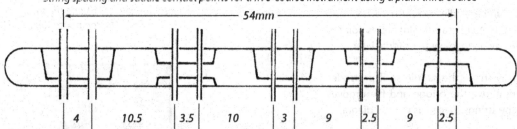

54mm

| 4 | 10.5 | 3.5 | 10 | 3 | 9 | 2.5 | 9 | 2.5 |

String spacing and saddle contact points for a five-course instrument using a wound third course

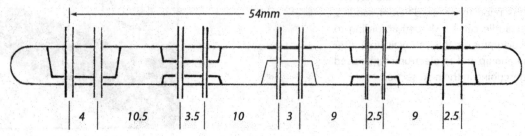

54mm

| 4 | 10.5 | 3.5 | 10 | 3 | 9 | 2.5 | 9 | 2.5 |

Setup

Strings for bouzoukis and citterns are always a problem. While a couple of string manufacturers do make pre-packaged sets it seems that many instruments require individually customised sets of strings that bring out the best in that particular instrument and suit the player's requirements.

My suggested gauges for a four course, 660mm (26") scale bouzouki are .010", .017", .030", .040".

For a four course, 580mm (22") scale octave mandolin gauges are .012", .018"p (or .020"w), .034", .046". A wound .020" string will require the saddle contact point to be in front of the contact point for the .012" string.

A five course 580mm (22") scale cittern will have a .009" string added as the top string.

Instruments of other scale lengths will need to have the string gauges calculated. Appendix 2 has the necessary formulas and graphs, or there are on-line calculators available.

Fit the strings and bring the instrument up to pitch. This might well take a few minutes until the tuning stabilises.

First check the neck for straightness. The tension may have put a bow into the neck. A straight edge along the centreline of the neck will show how much bow or 'relief' has been put into the neck. There are two schools of thought on neck relief - one for it and one against very much of it at all. The pro-relief line of thinking is that a slight bow - up to 1mm in the centre - is desirable for the strings to clear the higher frets when they are vibrating. I prefer less relief, between .25 and .5mm in the centre of the neck between the 1st fret and the body join.

Adjusting the amount of relief is the job of the trussrod. This can be done with the neck under string tension. Tighten the trussrod nut, while checking the relief with the straight edge.

Tightening the rod, and bending the neck back towards straightness will raise the pitch of the strings, so check the tuning after adjusting the rod. Once the neck has been set to the amount of relief desired, the nut height can be set.

The basic principle of setting the height of the nut, or at least the nut slots, is to avoid the strings hitting the first fret when played as open (ie, unfreted) strings. When the string is held down between the second and third fret, it should just clear the first fret. The clearance should just be the thickness of a sheet of paper, so that when the string is tapped over the first fret, there is a slight 'tink' as the string is pushed down to the fret. Any more clearance just means working too hard to fret the string, and if the string touches the first fret it will buzz when played as an open string.

Using the correct size nut files, slowly deepen each slot until the correct depth is reached. The slots should be at slightly less angle than the angle of the head to maintain down pressure in the nut slot. Each string can be lifted out of its slot in turn, while keeping the string tension to the correct pitch.

Once the nut slots are filed correctly, check the action at the 12th fret. A good action to aim for is 5/64" on the treble strings and 6/64" on the bass strings and an even change across the middle courses. With the saddle initially cut high, the action is likely to be higher than this, so for each 1/64" that the strings are too high, 1/32" should be removed from the saddle.

I warned you that I used a combination of metric and imperial measurements, but this has always been a useful way to set the action, as even being half a 64th too high at the twelfth fret means just taking a 64th off the saddle. Small metal rulers that measure 64th of an inch are easily available as well.

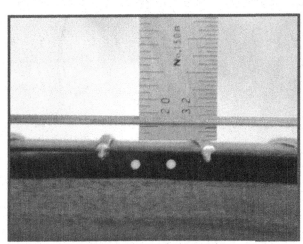

Checking the action at the 12th fret

Either the bottom of the saddle can be reduced or the shape of the top can be modified. Pencil marks down the front of the saddle in line with the grooves will help to re-file them. The finished saddle should be close to 3mm (or 8/64") above the top of the bridge if the top of the bridge itself is in line with the top of the frets.

The diagram shows how the saddle should be shaped for string compensation using the suggested gauges. Using a wound second course (or third course for the five course instrument) of .018 -.020" will mean a different shape as shown in the second diagram.

The measurements given here are approximations. The most accurate way to do this is with an electronic tuner, and a small piece of wire (the cut off bit of a thick plain string is good) as the contact point on the saddle, moving the contact point back and forwards until the harmonic at the twelfth fret matches the fretted note. Make the correct contact points with a pencil and de-tune the instrument to remove the saddle and file ramps up to the contact points. It looks better to start the ramps at the point where the saddle protrudes from the bridge itself. The flat sections on the top of the saddle should be about 2mm wide if possible, though the bottom G string may want to be further back and reduce this. The string grooves should be slightly reshaped to angle back slightly from the front of the groove towards the back.

Polish the saddle in the same way as the nut, re-insert it in the slot, tune the instrument up and start playing.

Opposite page:
The 580mm (22") scale cittern built for
this book. The soundboard is moulded
Englemann spruce, the back, sides and neck
are Tasmanian blackwood, with Indian
rosewood binding and ebony fingerboard,
bridge and tailpiece

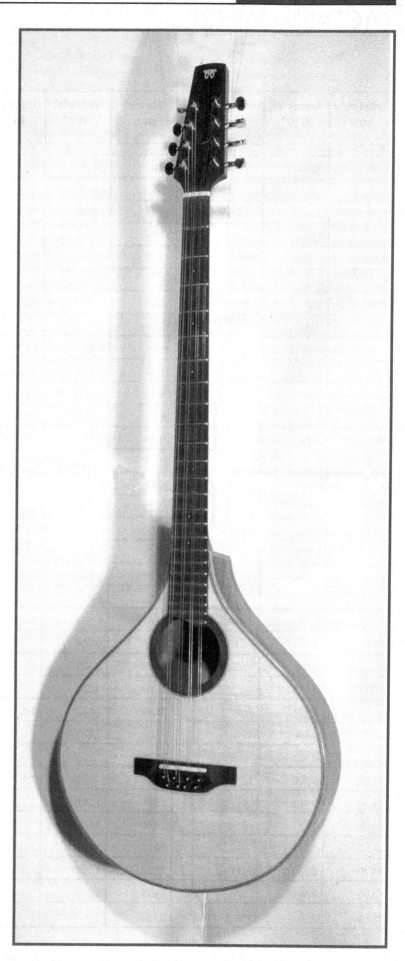

The 660mm (26") scale bouzouki also built while
writing the book. It has an Englemann spruce
soundboard, with the body and neck made from
Queensland walnut (Endiandra palmerstoni).
The bindings are flamed maple and the
fingerboard and bridge are ebony.

METRIC/IMPERIAL

Metric mm	Imperial .000"	Imperial inch		Metric mm	Imperial .000"	Imperial inch		Metric mm	Imperial .000"	Imperial inch
0.79	0.031	1/32"		15.88	0.625	5/8"		33.00	1.299	
1.00	0.039			16.00	0.630			33.34	1.313	1-5/16"
1.59	0.062	1/16"		16.67	0.656	21/32"		34.00	1.339	
2.00	0.079			17.00	0.669			34.93	1.375	1-3/8"
2.38	0.094	3/32"		17.46	0.688	11/16"		35.00	1.378	
3.00	0.118			18.00	0.709			36.00	1.417	
3.18	0.125	1/8"		18.26	0.719	23/32"		36.51	1.437	1-7/16"
3.97	0.156	5/32"		19.00	0.748			37.00	1.457	
4.00	0.157			19.05	0.750	3/4"		38.00	1.496	
4.76	0.188	3/16"		19.84	0.781	25/32"		38.10	1.500	1-1/2"
5.00	0.197			20.00	0.787			39.00	1.535	
5.56	0.219	7/32"		20.64	0.813	13/16"		39.69	1.563	1-9/16"
6.00	0.236			21.00	0.827			40.00	1.575	
6.35	0.250	1/4"		21.43	0.844	27/32"		41.00	1.614	
7.00	0.276			22.00	0.866			41.28	1.625	1-5/8"
7.14	0.281	9/32"		22.23	0.875	7/8"		42.00	1.654	
7.94	0.313	5/16"		23.00	0.906			42.86	1.687	1-11/16"
8.00	0.315			23.02	0.906	29/32"		43.00	1.693	
8.73	0.344	11/32"		23.81	0.938	15/16"		44.00	1.732	
9.00	0.354			24.00	0.945			44.45	1.750	1-3/4"
9.53	0.375	3/8"		24.61	0.969	31/32"		45.00	1.772	
10.00	0.394			25.00	0.984			46.00	1.811	
10.32	0.406	13/32"		25.40	1.000	1"		46.04	1.813	1-13/16"
11.00	0.433			26.00	1.024			47.00	1.850	
11.11	0.438	7/16"		26.99	1.063	1-1/16"		47.63	1.875	1-7/8"
11.91	0.469	15/32"		27.00	1.063			48.00	1.890	
12.00	0.472			28.00	1.102			49.00	1.929	
12.70	0.500	1/2"		28.58	1.125	1-1/8"		49.21	1.937	1-15/16"
13.00	0.512			29.00	1.142			50.00	1.969	
13.49	0.531	17/32"		30.00	1.181			50.80	2.000	2"
14.00	0.551			30.16	1.187	1-3/16"		53.98	2.125	2-1/8"
14.29	0.563	9/16"		31.00	1.220			55.00	2.165	
15.00	0.591			31.75	1.250	1-1/4"		57.15	2.250	2-1/4"
15.08	0.594	19/32"		32.00	1.260			60.00	2.362	

mm	inches			mm	inches			mm	inches	
60.33	2.375	2-3/8"		127.00	5.000	5"		240.00	9.449	
63.50	2.500	2-1/2"		130.00	5.118			241.30	9.500	9-1/2"
65.00	2.559			133.35	5.250	5-1/4"		250.00	9.843	
66.68	2.625	2-5/8"		135.00	5.315			254.00	10.000	10"
69.85	2.750	2-3/4"		139.70	5.500	5-1/2"		260.00	10.236	
70.00	2.756			140.00	5.512			270.00	10.630	
73.03	2.875	2-7/8"		145.00	5.709			279.40	11.000	11"
75.00	2.953			146.05	5.750	5-3/4"		280.00	11.024	
76.20	3.000	3"		150.00	5.906			290.00	11.417	
80.00	3.150			152.40	6.000	6"		300.00	11.811	
82.55	3.250	3-1/4"		158.75	6.250	6-1/4"		304.80	12.000	12"
85.00	3.346			160.00	6.299			330.20	13.000	13"
88.90	3.500	3-1/2"		165.10	6.500	6-1/2"		355.60	14.000	14"
90.00	3.543			170.00	6.693			381.00	15.000	15"
95.00	3.740			171.45	6.750	6-3/4"		406.40	16.000	16"
95.25	3.750	3-3/4"		177.80	7.000	7"		431.80	17.000	17"
100.00	3.937			180.00	7.087			457.20	18.000	18"
101.60	4.000	4"		190.00	7.480			482.60	19.000	19"
105.00	4.134			190.50	7.500	7-1/2"		508.00	20.000	20"
107.95	4.250	4-1/4"		200.00	7.874			533.40	21.000	21"
110.00	4.331			203.20	8.000	8"		558.80	22.000	22"
114.30	4.500	4-1/2"		210.00	8.268			584.20	23.000	23"
115.00	4.528			215.90	8.500	8-1/2"		609.60	24.000	24"
120.00	4.724			220.00	8.661			635.00	25.000	25"
120.65	4.750	4-3/4"		228.60	9.000	9"		660.40	26.000	26"
125.00	4.921			230.00	9.055			685.80	27.000	27"

American string manufacturers measures their strings guages in thousandths of an inch, while European manuafcturers use millimetres. To convert inches into mm multiply by 25.4 - similarly, to convert mm into inches, divide by 25.4.

inches	mm	inches	mm	inches	mm	inches	mm	inches	mm
.007	0.18	.019	0.48	.031	0.79	.043	1.09	.055	1.40
.008	0.20	.020	0.51	.032	0.81	.044	1.12	.056	1.42
.009	0.23	.021	0.53	.033	0.84	.045	1.14	.057	1.45
.010	0.25	.022	0.56	.034	0.86	.046	1.17	.058	1.47
.011	0.28	.023	0.58	.035	0.89	.047	1.19	.059	1.50
.012	0.30	.024	0.61	.036	0.91	.048	1.22	.060	1.52
.013	0.33	.025	0.64	.037	0.94	.049	1.24	.070	1.78
.014	0.36	.026	0.66	.038	0.97	.050	1.27	.080	2.03
.015	0.38	.027	0.69	.039	0.99	.051	1.30	.090	2.29
.016	0.41	.028	0.71	.040	1.02	.052	1.32	.100	2.54
.017	0.43	.029	0.74	.041	1.04	.053	1.35	.110	2.79
.018	0.46	.030	0.76	.042	1.07	.054	1.37	.120	2.82

Back many years ago the Guild of American Luthiers published as Data Sheet 144, from Max Krimmel, the following formula:

$$T = 4 \times F^2 \times L \times M / 980621$$

where

T = Tension in Kgs
F = Frequency in Hz
L = Vibrating string length in cm
M = Mass of that length in gm
980621 is a constant which has something to do with gravity (don't ask me, I have no idea).

If you want to work out the gauges of strings for a predetermined scale length and tension the formula becomes:

$$M = 980621 \times T / 4 \times F^2 \times L$$

The tricky thing to know is what tension you want for any particular instrument. This is a matter of both trial & error and personal preference, but a good starting point are D'Addario string packets which now give the tension for each string for a standard guitar scale length at common pitches For example a light gauge guitar set has string tensions of 10-12 kgs per string, and that is probably a good starting point.

Of course the information that is critical for applying this formula is the string mass, so over a period of a few weeks every time I restrung an instrument I cut off 10cm from the end of the strings. The strings came from a number of manufacturers, and both plain steel and wound strings were accumulated. The wound strings had a variety of wrap compositions (brass, bronze, phosphor bronze), but neither this nor the manufacturer seemed to make much difference to the mass of the string.

The Powerhouse Museum in Sydney kindly let me weigh the bits of string in their lab, and these were plotted into graphs .

Plain steel strings

Gauge	Mass in gm per 10cm
.008"	.025
.009	.03
.010	.04
.011	.048
.012	.057
.013	.065
.015	.09
.016	.102
.017	.114
.018	.135
.020	.162
.022	.193
.024	.231

Wound Strings

Gauge	Mass in gm per 10cm
.020"	.17
.025	.225
.026	.25
.027	.275
.030	.325
.034	.45
.039	.525
.042	.625
.046	.75
.049	.835
.052	.96
.054	1.075
.056	1.16

The graphs on the next page show quite a smooth curve for both kinds of string, which makes reading information off them quite simple.

Here are a couple of examples of calulation that can be made:

Finding the tension of a .012" string tuned to E on a 63cm (24.8")scale instrument.

F = 329.6 Hz $F^2 = 108636.16$
L = 63
M = .057 x 6.3 = .359gm

T = 4 x 108636.16 x 63 x .359 / 980621
= 10.02 Kg or 22.05lb

Finding gauge of string required for 110Hz A (guitar fifth) at a tension of 7kg for a 66cm scale

T = 7 Kg
F = 110 Hz $F^2 = 12100$
L = 66 cm

M = 980621 x 7 / 4 x 12100 x 66
= 2.15gm   divide this by 6.6
= 3.3gm and from the graph the string required is a .030" wound string.

The other information required is a table of pitches and frequencies

E = 82.407 Hz (guitar 6th)
F = 87.307
F#= 92.499
G = 97.999
G#= 103.826
A = 110 (guitar 5th)
A#= 116.541
B = 123.471
C = 130.813
C#= 138.591
D = 146.832 (guitar 4th)
D#= 155.563

This was originally published in *American Lutherie* No 2 June 1985. The Guild of American Luthiers is a fine organization and their quarterly journal is essential reading for any stringed instrument builder. There are now a number of websites which will calculate this information in amatter of seconds.

Plain Strings

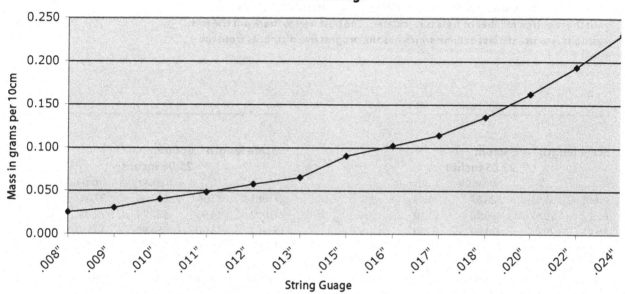

Wound Strings

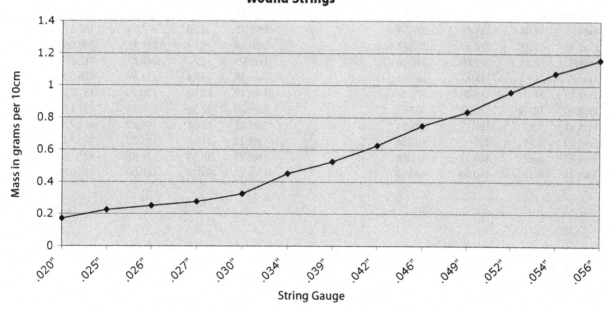

alculating the distance between frets is a simple mathmatical exercise. The scale length is devided by 17.817, and the result is the distance to the first fret. That is subtracted from the scale length and the division repeated until the required number of frets is calculated. The best way to mark out the fret positions is to use the last column which has the progressive distances from the nut.

Scale length - 560mm
22.05 inches

		remainder	from nut
Fret 1	31.43	528.57	31.43
Fret 2	29.67	498.90	61.10
Fret 3	28.00	470.90	89.10
Fret 4	26.43	444.47	115.53
Fret 5	24.95	419.52	140.48
Fret 6	23.55	395.98	164.02
Fret 7	22.22	373.75	186.25
Fret 8	20.98	352.78	207.22
Fret 9	19.80	332.98	227.02
Fret 10	18.69	314.29	245.71
Fret 11	17.64	296.65	263.35
Fret 12	16.65	280.00	280.00
Fret 13	15.72	264.28	295.72
Fret 14	14.83	249.45	310.55
Fret 15	14.00	235.45	324.55
Fret 16	13.21	222.23	337.77
Fret 17	12.47	209.76	350.24
Fret 18	11.77	197.99	362.01
Fret 19	11.11	186.88	373.12
Fret 20	10.49	176.39	383.61
Fret 21	9.90	166.49	393.51
Fret 22	9.34	157.14	402.86
Fret 23	8.82	148.32	411.68
Fret 24	8.32	140.00	420.00

Scale length - 660mm
25.98 inches

		remainder	from nut
Fret 1	37.04	622.96	37.04
Fret 2	34.96	587.99	72.01
Fret 3	33.00	554.99	105.01
Fret 4	31.15	523.84	136.16
Fret 5	29.40	494.44	165.56
Fret 6	27.75	466.69	193.31
Fret 7	26.19	440.50	219.50
Fret 8	24.72	415.77	244.23
Fret 9	23.34	392.44	267.56
Fret 10	22.03	370.41	289.59
Fret 11	20.79	349.62	310.38
Fret 12	19.62	330.00	330.00
Fret 13	18.52	311.48	348.52
Fret 14	17.48	293.99	366.01
Fret 15	16.50	277.49	382.51
Fret 16	15.57	261.92	398.08
Fret 17	14.70	247.22	412.78
Fret 18	13.88	233.34	426.66
Fret 19	13.10	220.25	439.75
Fret 20	12.36	207.88	452.12
Fret 21	11.67	196.22	463.78
Fret 22	11.01	185.20	474.80
Fret 23	10.39	174.81	485.19
Fret 24	9.81	165.00	495.00

Suggested reading

Williams, Jim. *A Guitar Maker's Manual.* Hal Leonard Publishing, 1986

Gore, Trevor & Gilet, Gerard. Contemporary Acoustic Guitar, Gore Guitars, 2011

Cumpiano, William R. & Natelson, Johnathan D. *Guitarmaking, tradition and technology.* Rosewood Press, 1987

Benedetto, Robert. *Making an Archtop Guitar.* Limelight Press 1994

McDonald, Graham. The Mandolin Project, McDonald Stringed Instruments, 2008

Siminoff, Roger H. *Constructing a Bluegrass Mandolin*. Hal Leonard Publishing, 1981

Troughton, John. *The Mandolin Manual.* Crowood Press, 2002

American Lutherie. Journal of the Guild of American Luthiers, 8222 South Park, Tacoma, WA 98408

Guitarmaker. Journal of the Association of Stringed Instrument Artisans, 1394 Stage Road, Richmond, VT 05477

Suppliers of Materials and Parts

This not an exhustive list, but those from whom I have bought wood and various tools and hardware over the years. All are virtually a 'one stop shop' for everything needed to build an instrument.

Gilet Guitars
Supplies most of the standard tonewoods and guitar parts, as well as being a good source of Tasmanian blackwood (aka black acacia)
4/6 Boralee St, Botany, NSW, 2019, Australia ph 02 9316 7467 (within Australia) or +612 9316 7467 (outside Australia)
www.giletguitars.com.au

Stewart- MacDonald
One of the main wood, parts, tools and kit suppliers.
Phone toll-free in USA & Canada 800 848 2273 www.stewmac.com

Luthiers Mercantile
The other major wood, parts, tools and kit suppliers.
PO Box 774, Healdsburg, CA, 95448 ph 800 477 4437 www.lmii.com

Allied Lutherie
Another supplier of wod, parts and tools.
PO Box 217, Healdsburg, CA, 95448 ph 707 431 3760
www.alliedlutherie.com

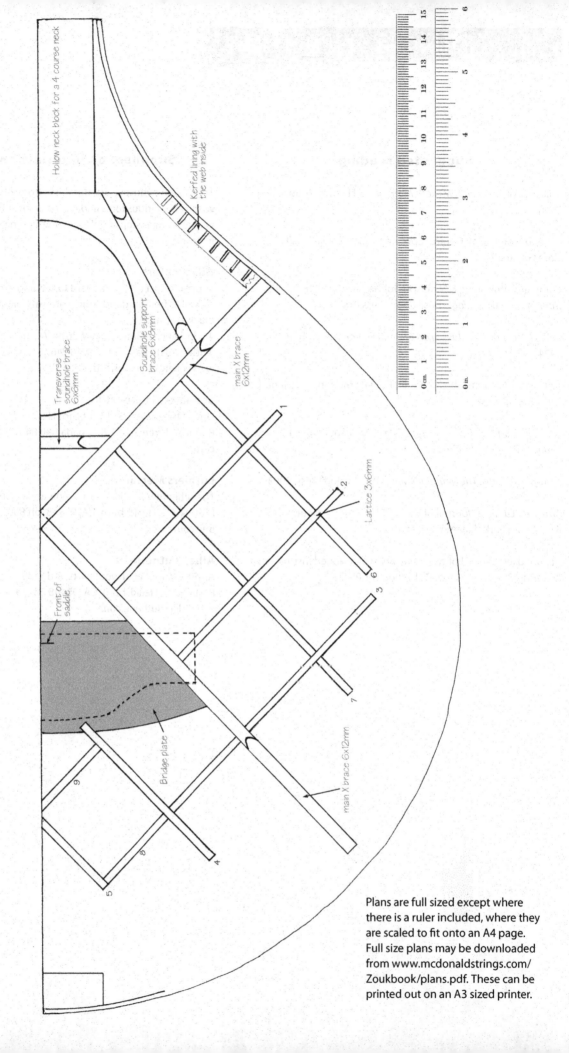

Hollow neck block for a 4 course neck

Kerfed lining with the web inside

Transverse soundhole brace 6x6mm

Soundhole support brace 6x6mm

main X brace 6x12mm

Lattice 3x6mm

Front of saddle

Bridge plate

main X brace 6x12mm

1
2
6
3
7
9
8
4
5

Plans are full sized except where there is a ruler included, where they are scaled to fit onto an A4 page. Full size plans may be downloaded from www.mcdonaldstrings.com/Zoukbook/plans.pdf. These can be printed out on an A3 sized printer.

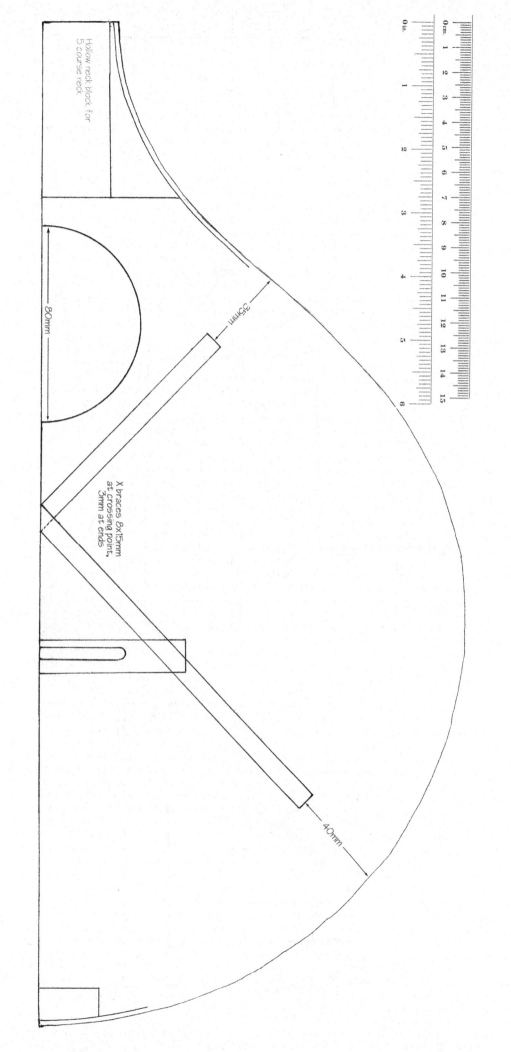

Hollow neck block for
5 course neck

80mm

35mm

X braces 8x15mm
at crossing point,
3mm at ends

40mm

Hollow neck block for
5 course neck

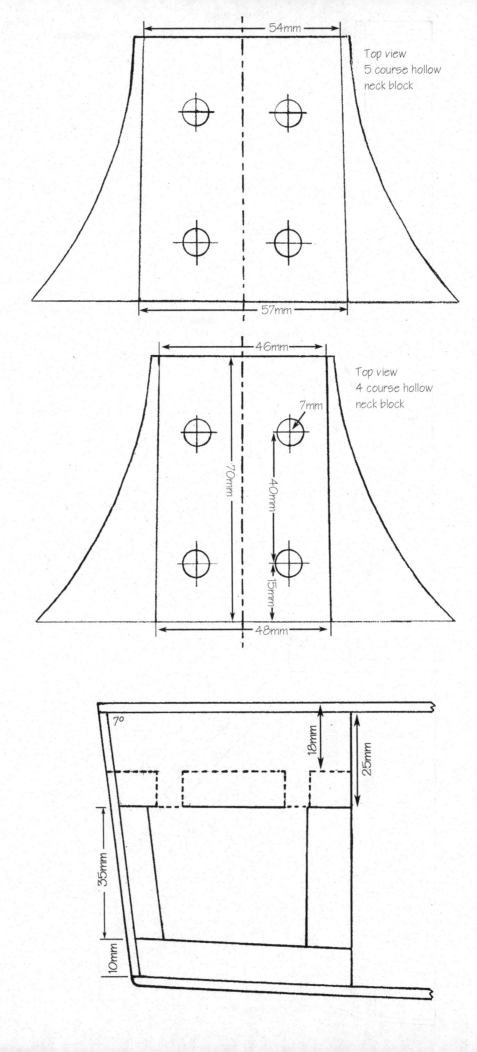

54mm

Top view
5 course hollow
neck block

57mm

46mm

Top view
4 course hollow
neck block

7mm

70mm

40mm

15mm

48mm

7°

18mm

25mm

35mm

10mm

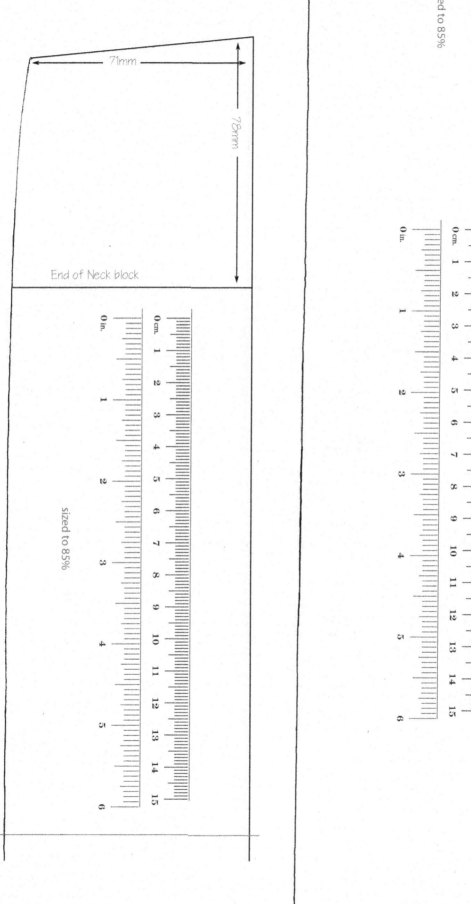

sized to 85%

Soundboard edge

81mm

71mm

78mm

End of Neck block

sized to 85%

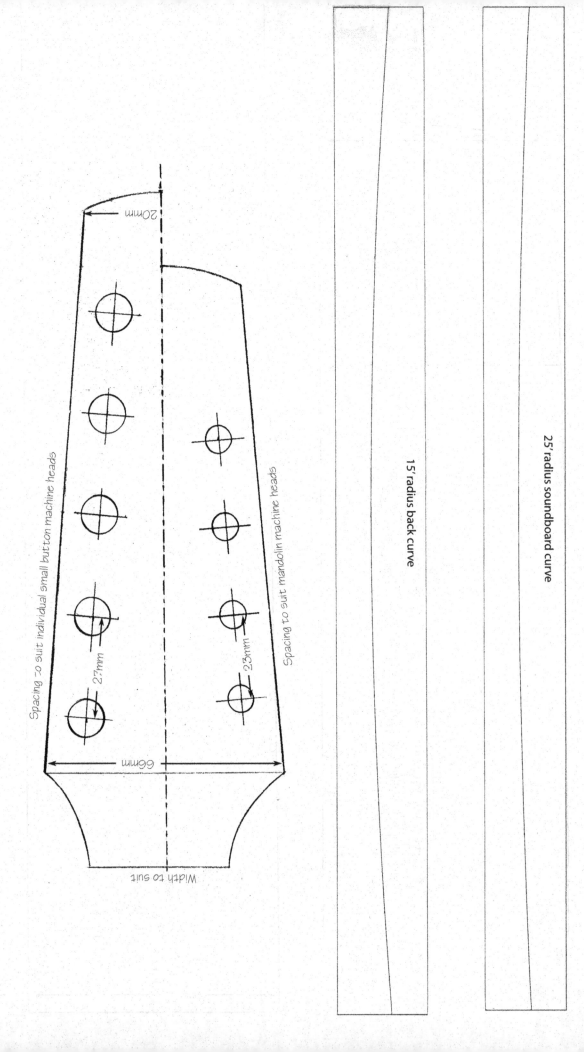

Spacing to suit individual small button machine heads

Spacing to suit mandolin machine heads

20mm

27mm

23mm

66mm

Width to suit

15' radius back curve

25' radius soundboard curve

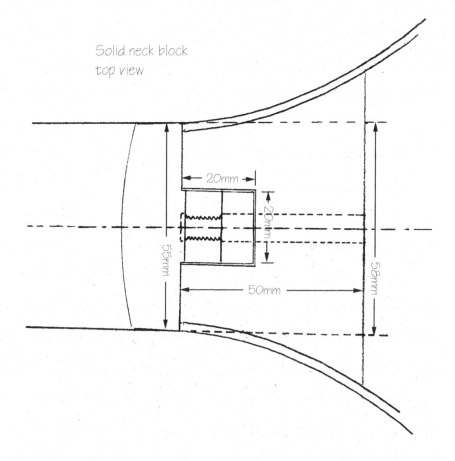

Solid neck block
top view

20mm

20mm

55mm

58mm

50mm

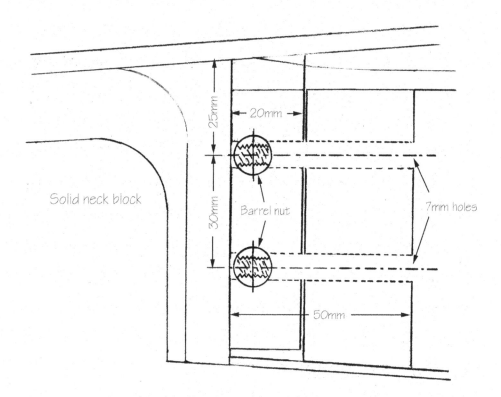

Solid neck block

25mm

20mm

30mm

Barrel nut

50mm

7mm holes